I MADE THESE DRAWINGS FOR YOU

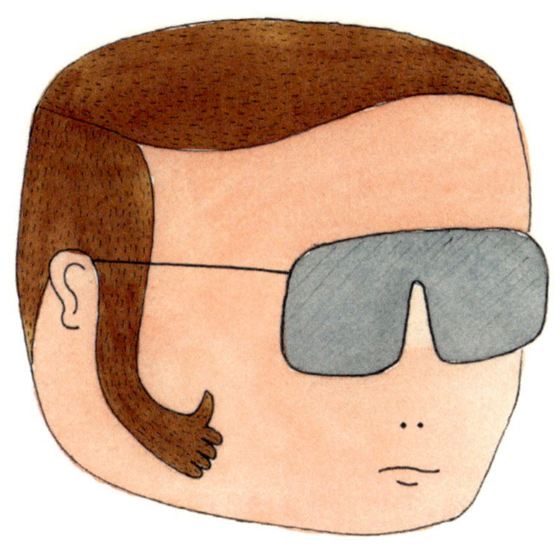

ABOUT THE ARTIST

Marc Johns grew up in the Eastern Townships of Quebec, Canada, in the small town of North Hatley, where he spent lots of time drawing. He received his Bachelors of Arts with Honours in Fine Arts from Bishop's University. He draws almost daily, and has been for as long as he can remember.

In 2006, Marc began sharing his artwork online, posting new work on a regular basis. His witty and thought-provoking drawings were quickly embraced, and earned him a fast-growing community of fans around the world. The rapidly expanding exposure has led to appearances in books and gallery exhibitions, features in magazines, commissions on CD covers, and a generous amount of attention on blogs.
Marc continues to share his prolific output online at **www.marcjohns.com**.

He lives in Victoria, Canada with his wife, two boys, and a drawer full of pens.

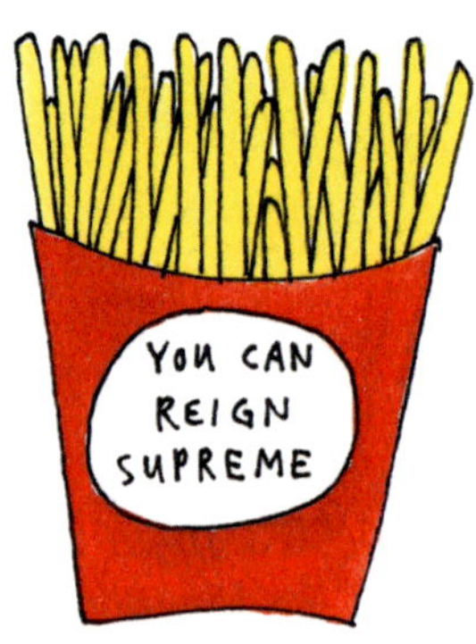

parallelogram books

CANADA

www.parallelogrambooks.com

ISBN: 978-0-9917205-0-7

Published just for you.

for Kristen, Ben and Sam

LOOK AT
THIS PAGE
FIRST.

OKAY. CARRY ON...

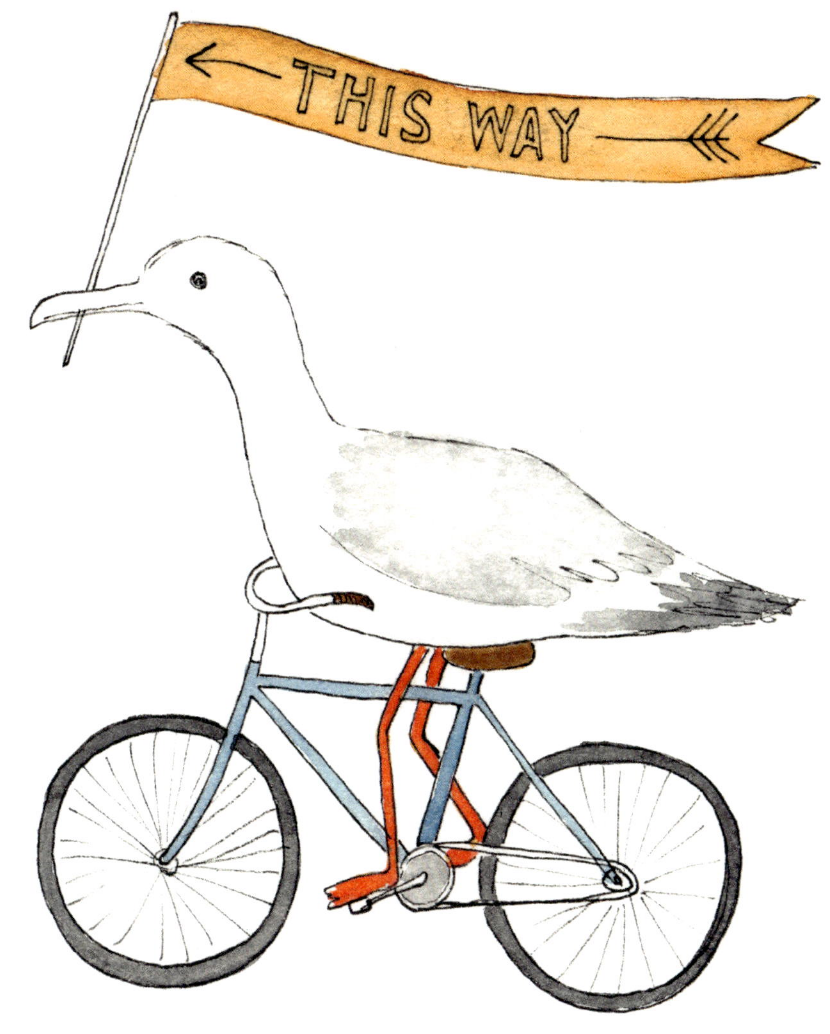

It's amazing we're able to get through the day
With no seagulls on bicycles, leading the way.

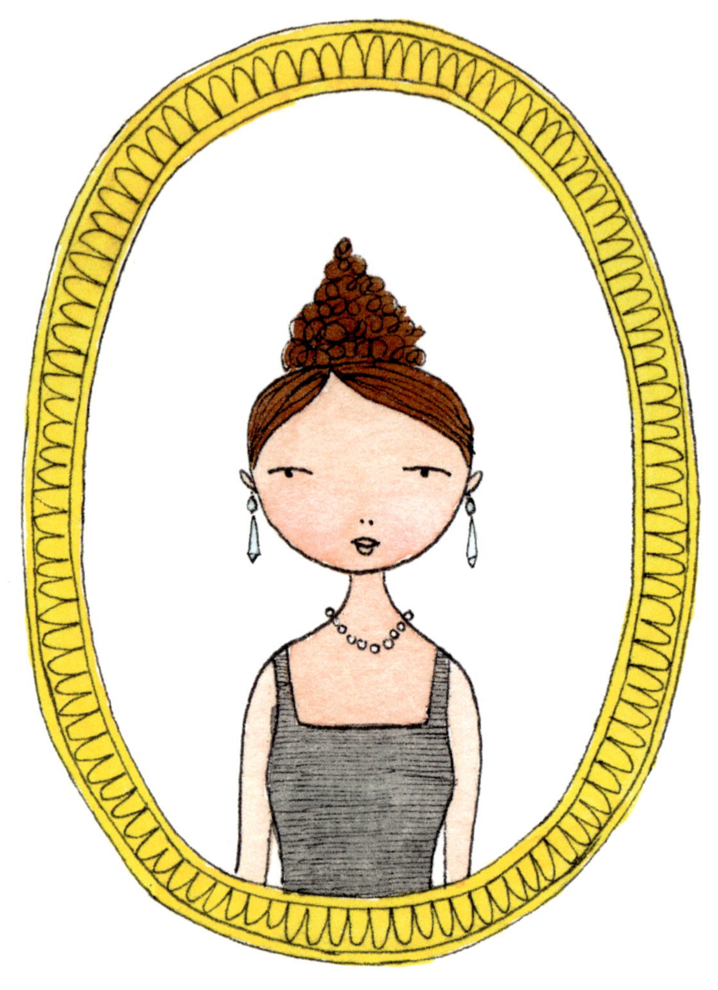

She felt rather classy
within the confines
of the oval frame.

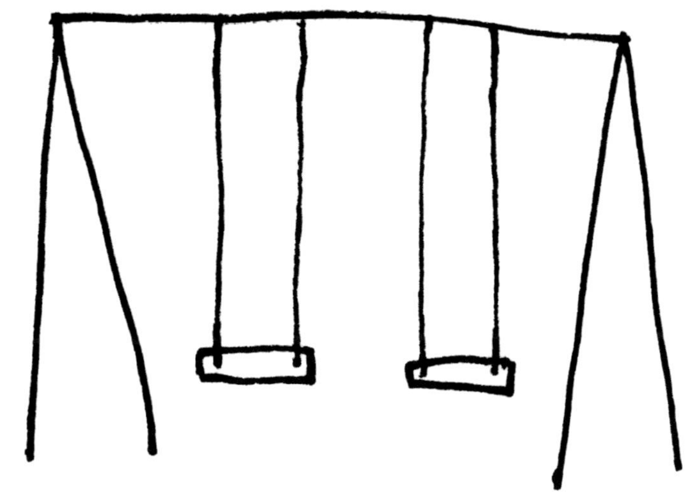

don't forget to play

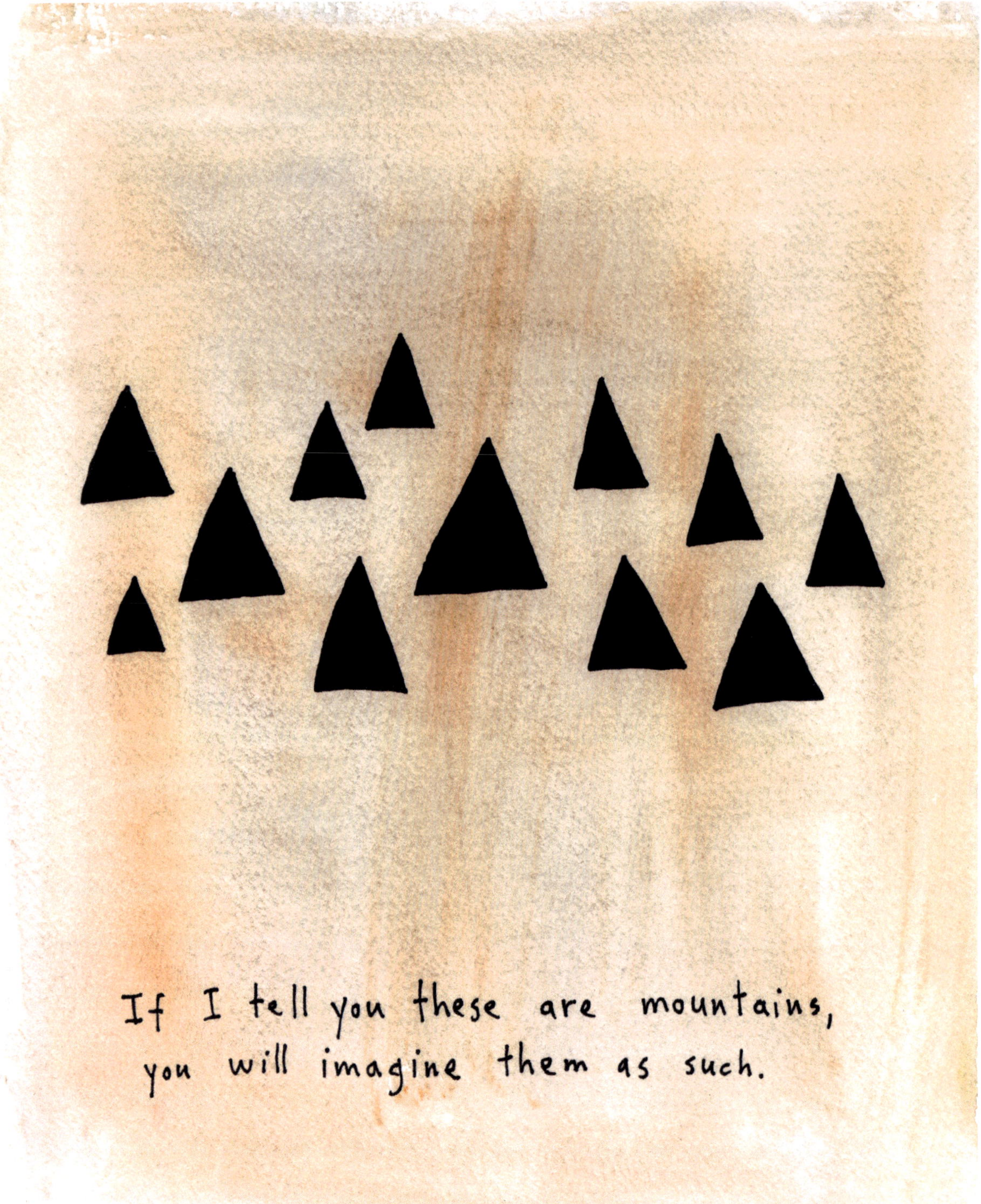

If I tell you these are mountains,
you will imagine them as such.

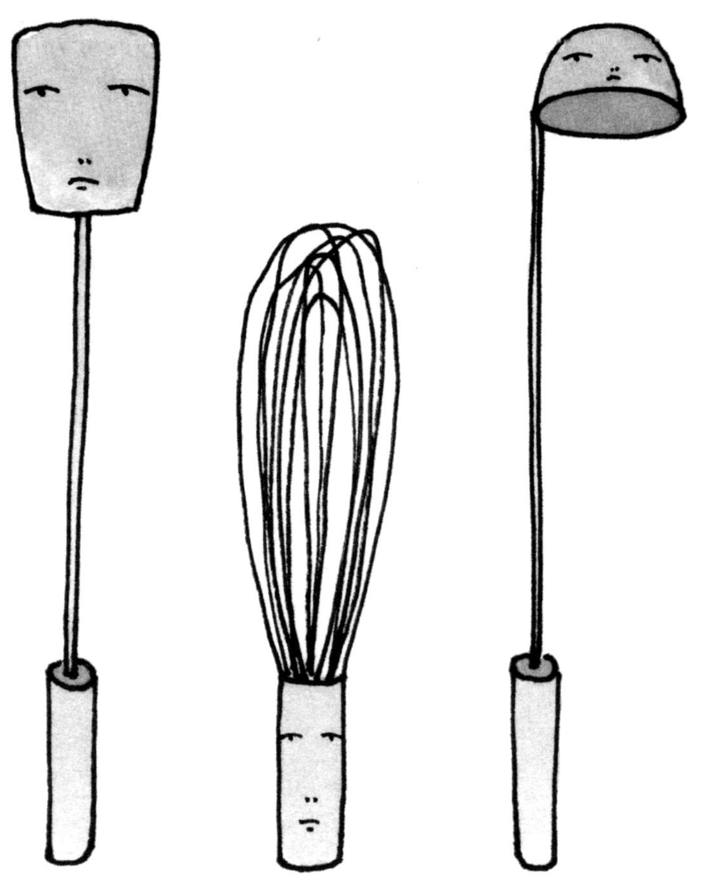

The whisk wasn't the tallest,
but he had terrific hair.

You stole my thunder,
But I stole your lightning.

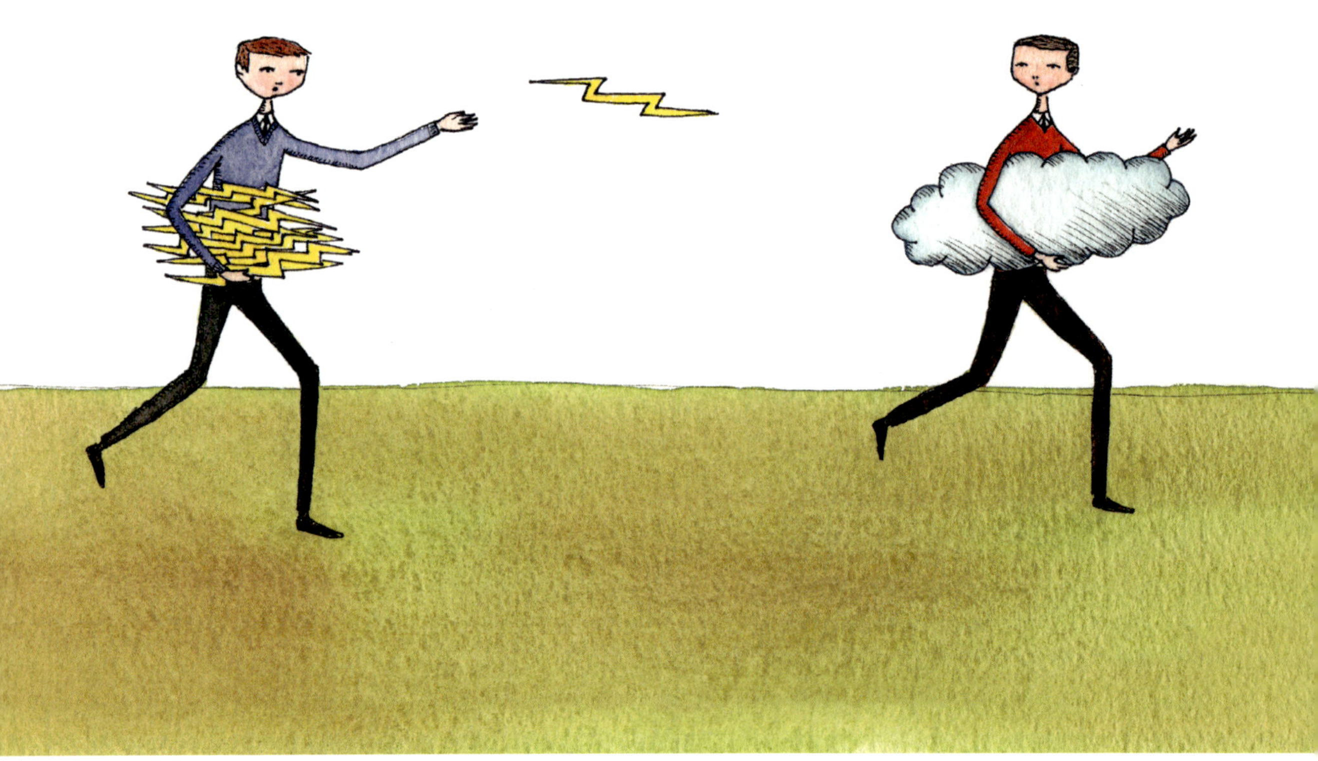

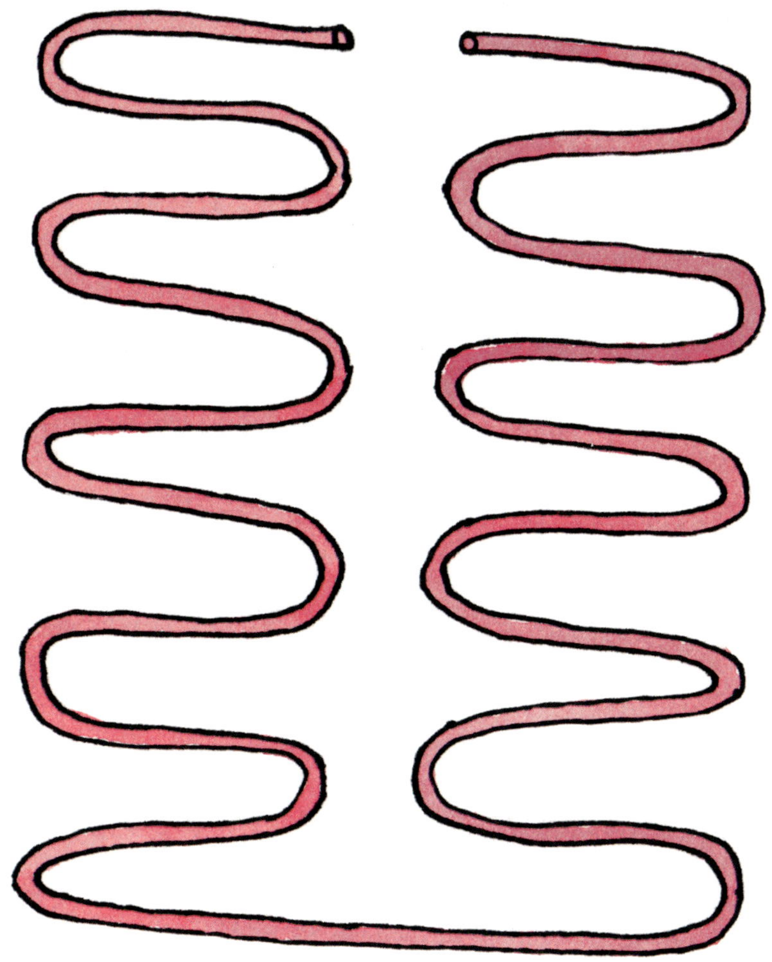

my intestine, arranged in a lovely pattern for you.

BUY THIS LIPSTICK

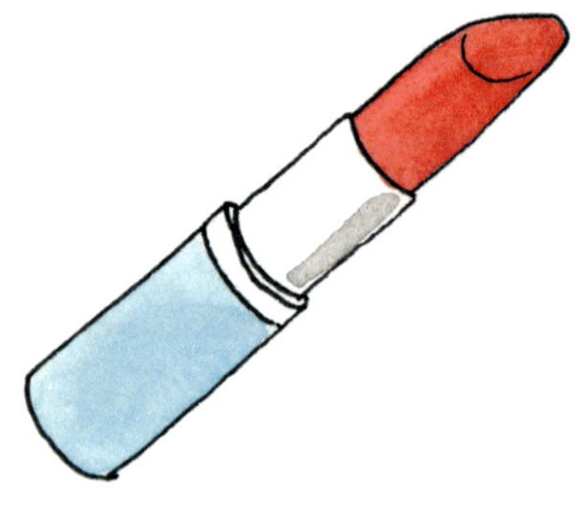

KISS GEORGE CLOONEY

BUY THIS TELEPHONE

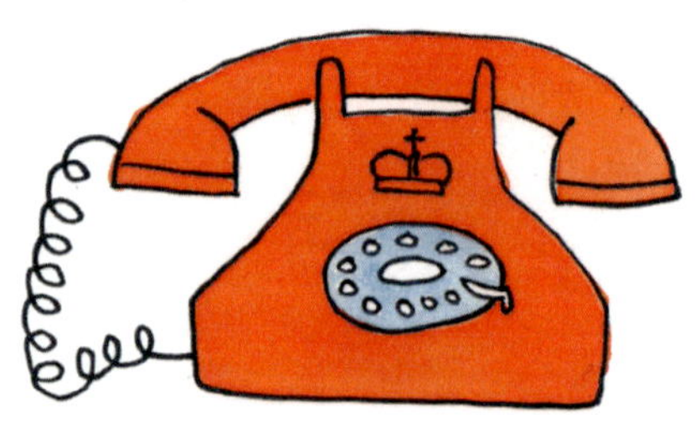

TALK TO THE QUEEN

BUY THIS SOUP

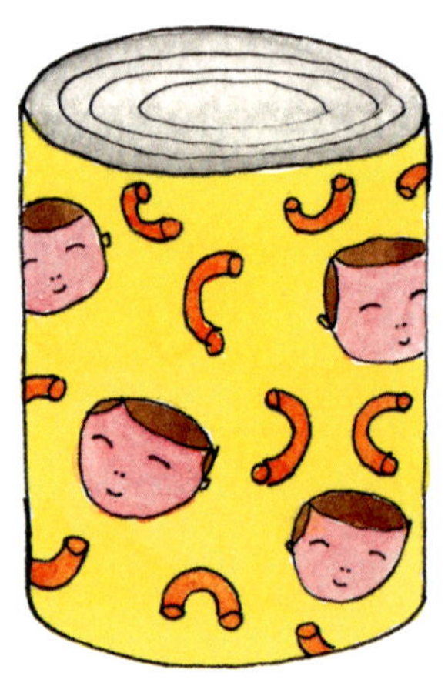

it has happy faces on the label

BUY THIS TIE

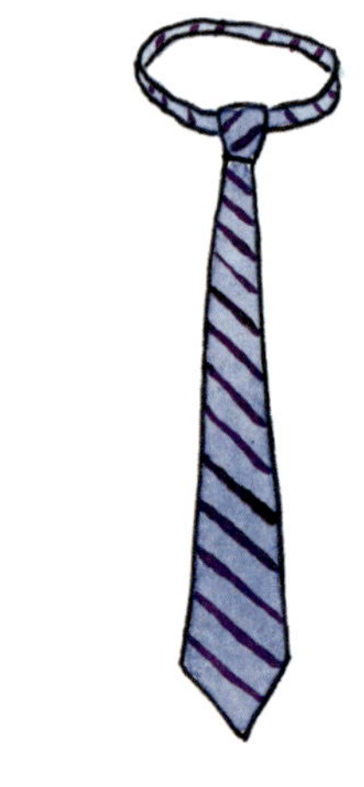

LOOK 23% SMARTER

BUY THIS CAR

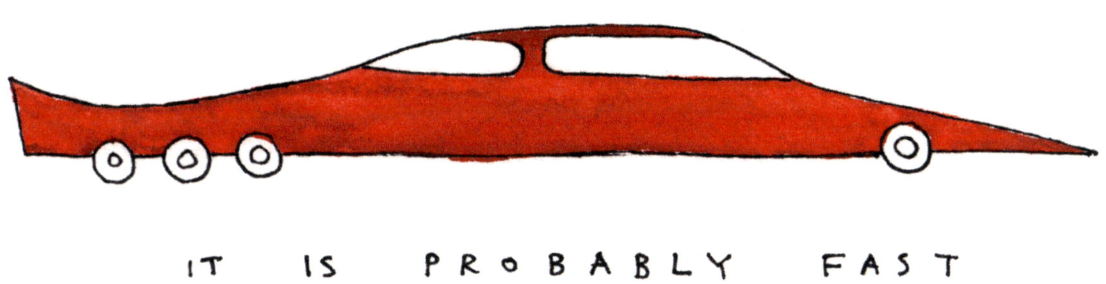

OKAY
LET'S
DO
THIS

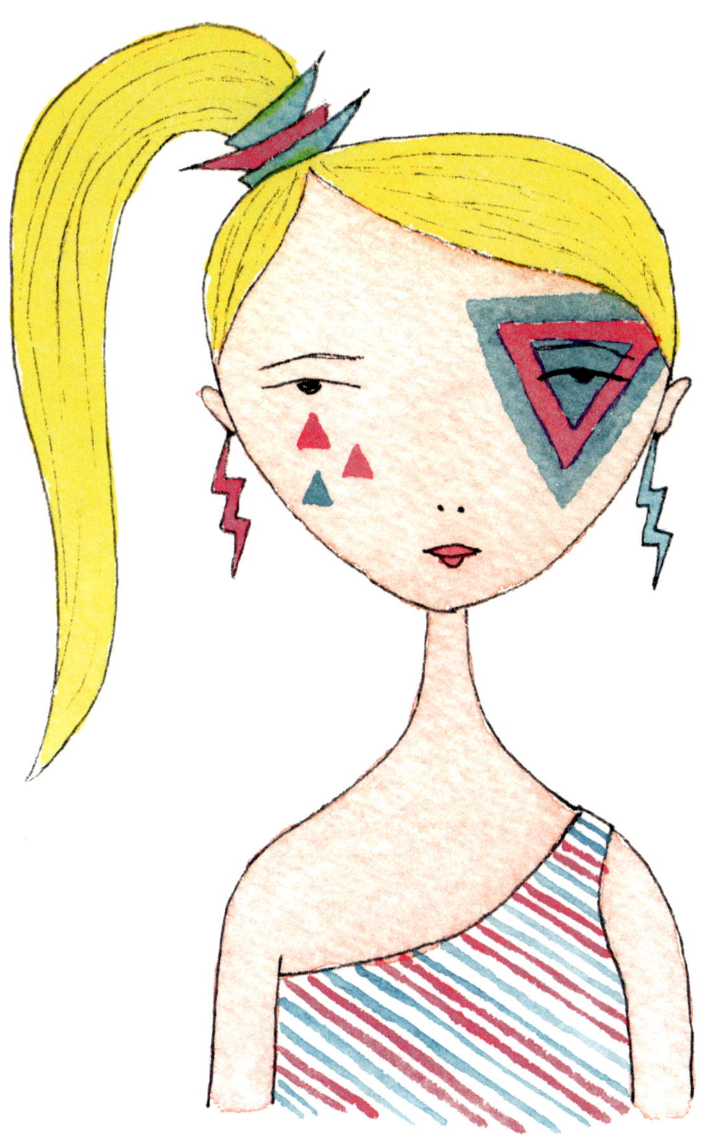

Her radness was evident.

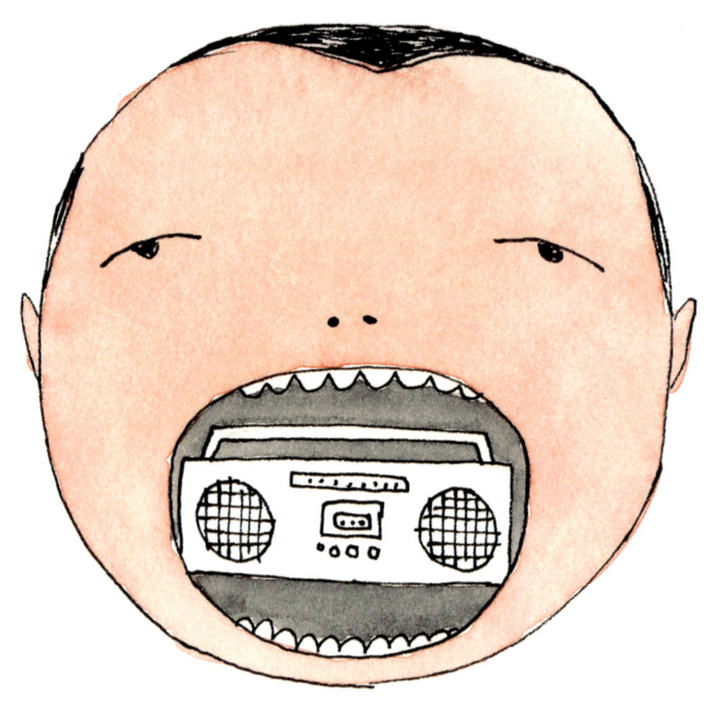

the music was inside him.

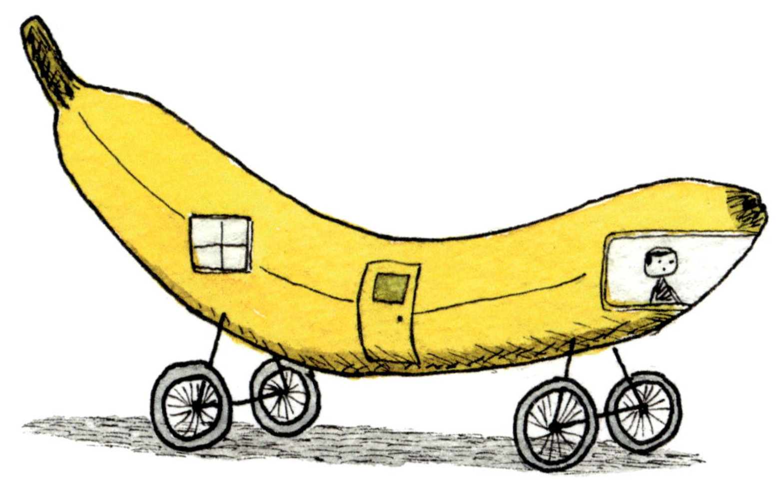

Bob was a cook
and delivered hot meals
He lived in a yellow
banana on wheels

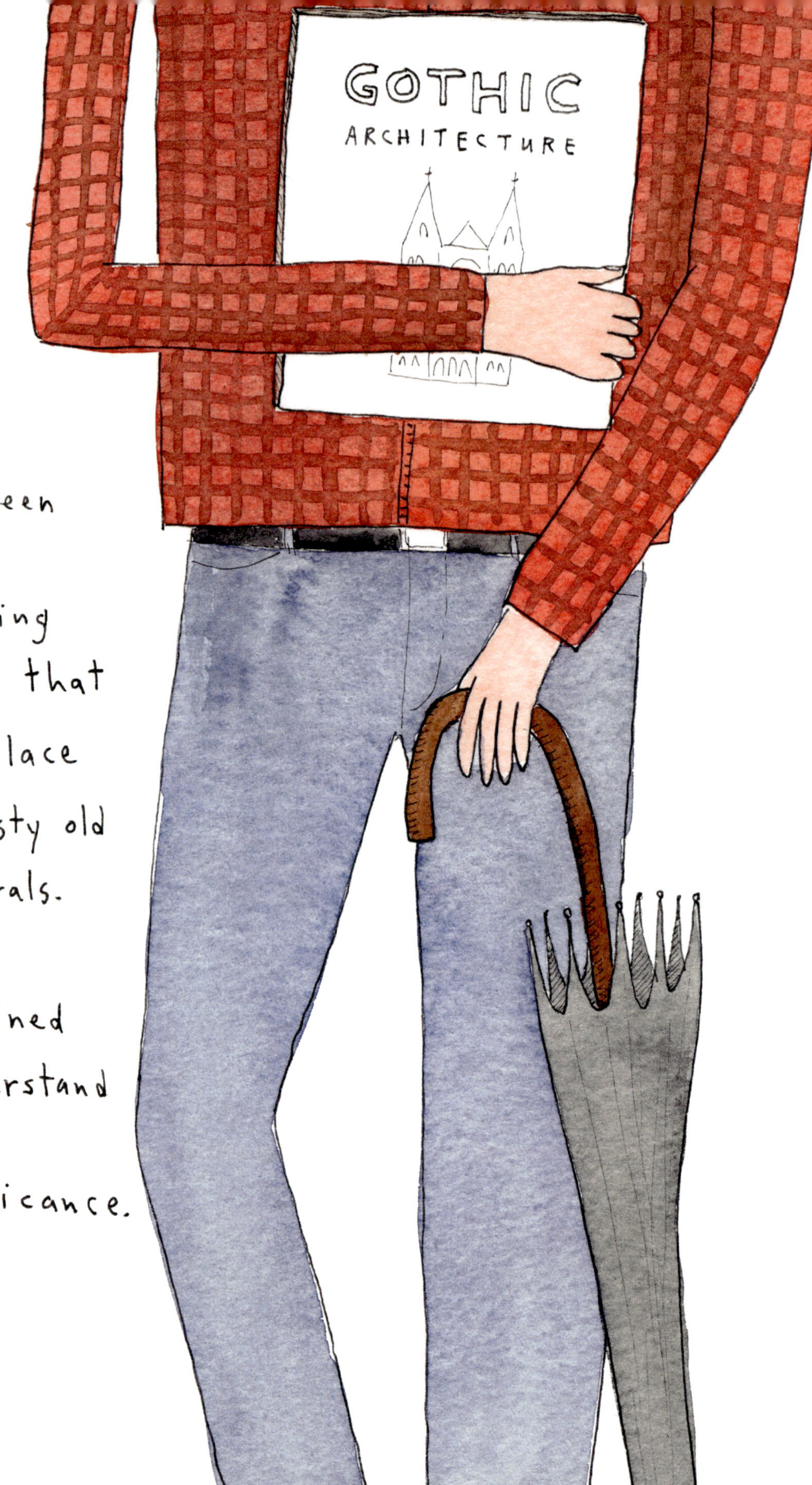

He'd been having recurring dreams that took place in musty old cathedrals. He was determined to understand their significance.

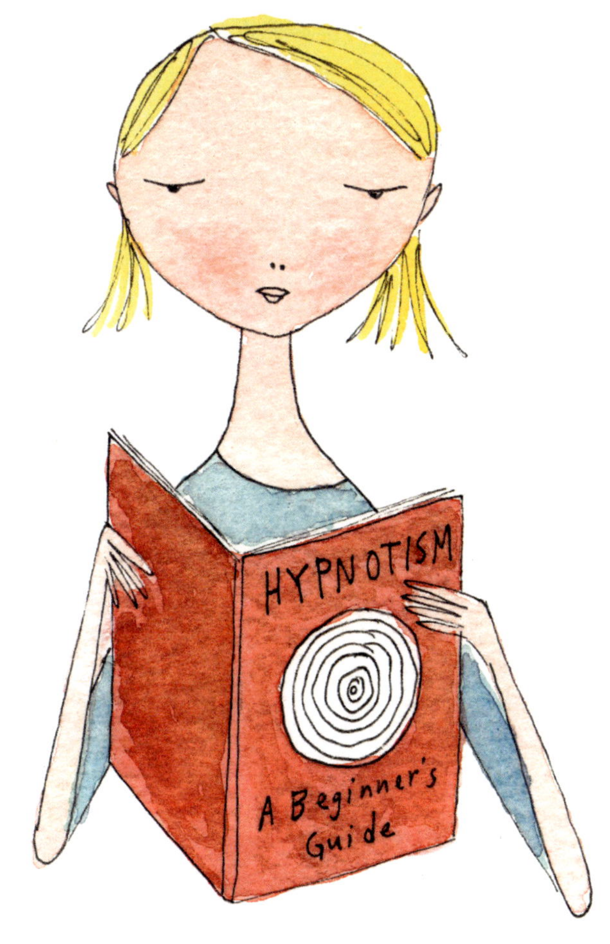

She was in love with Patrick. And if her efforts prove to be effective, he will soon be in love with her.

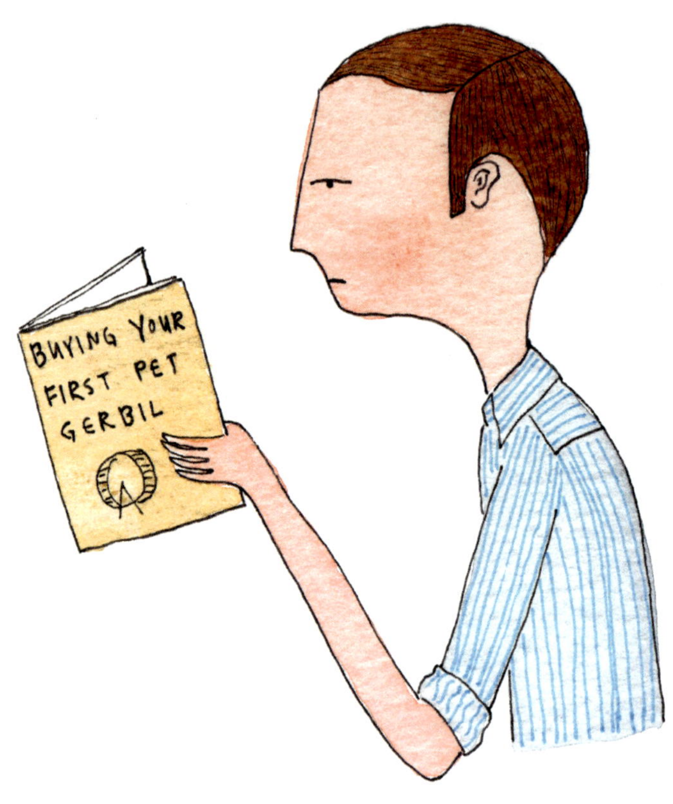

He was feeling particularly lonely.

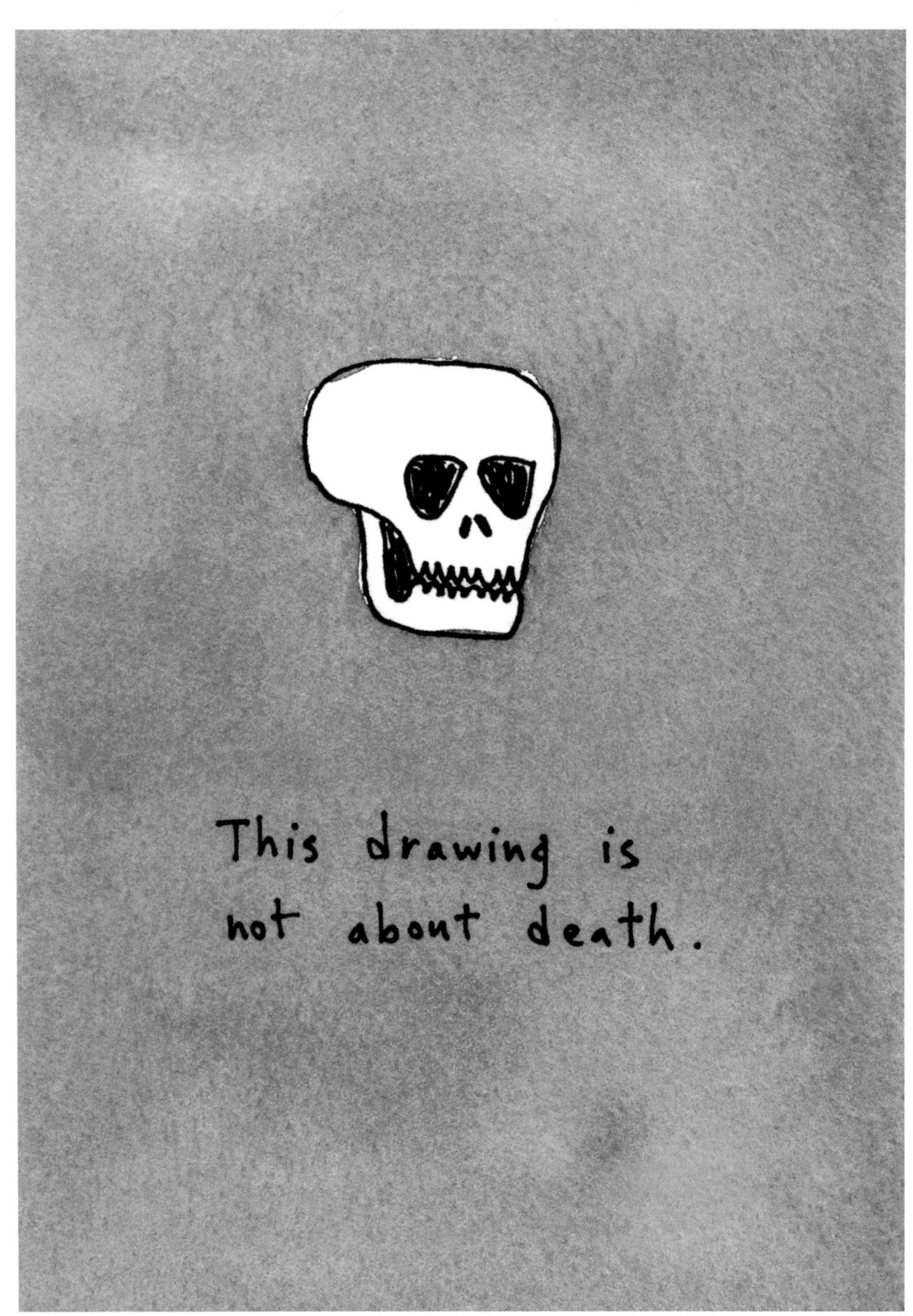
This drawing is
not about death.

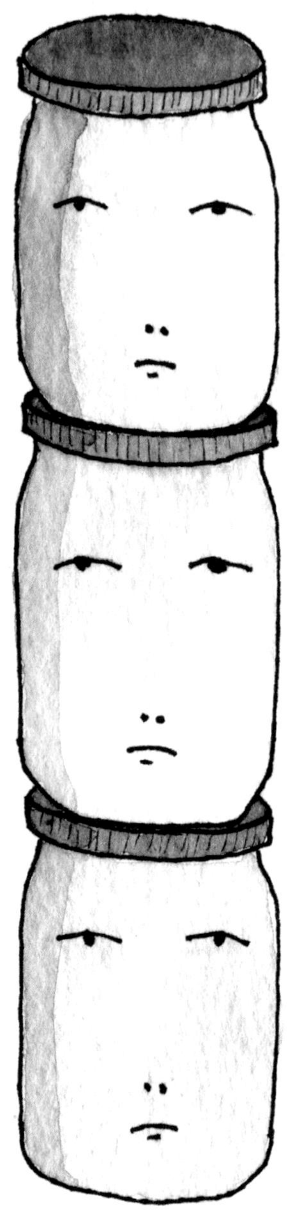

we are jars

we are better than you

because we are stackable

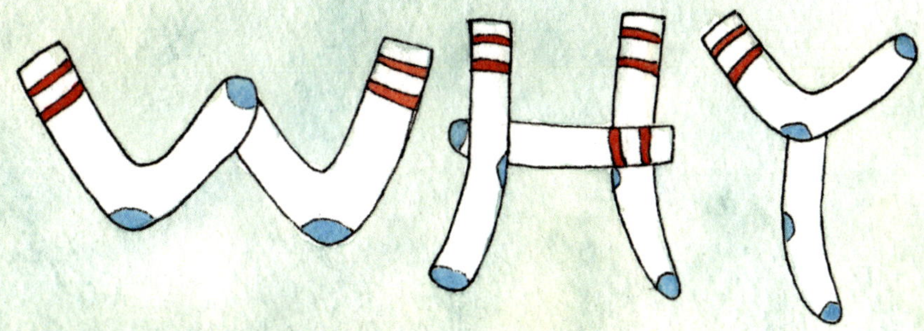

philosophically inquisitive gym socks

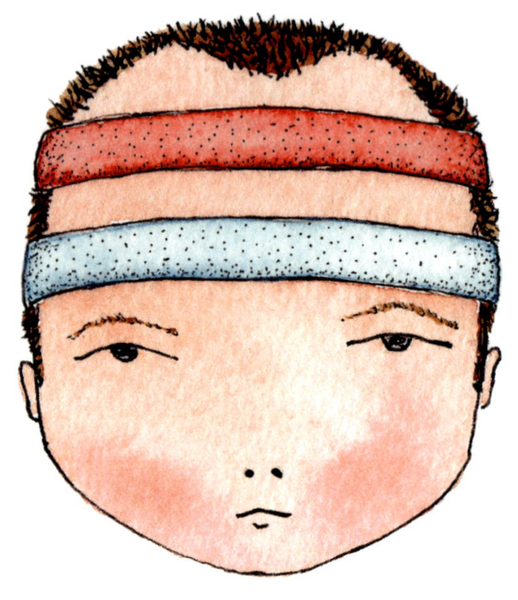

His large head allowed him to wear two headbands at once. He saw it as a distinct advantage.

zig zags were in vogue

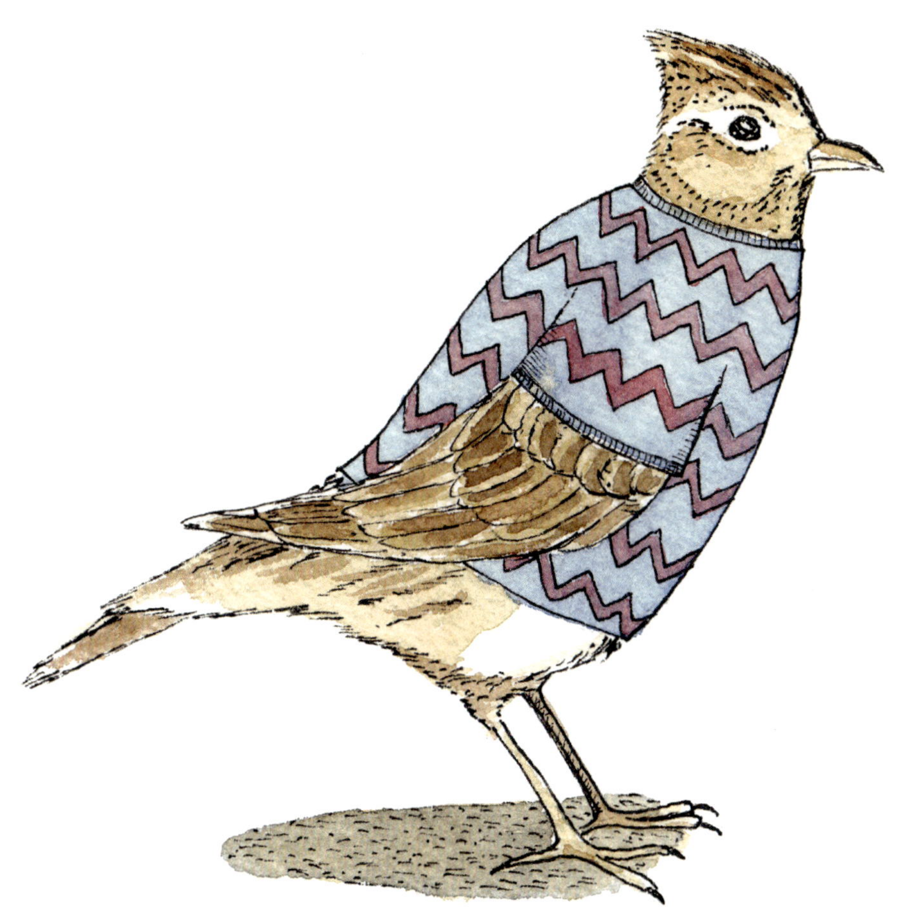

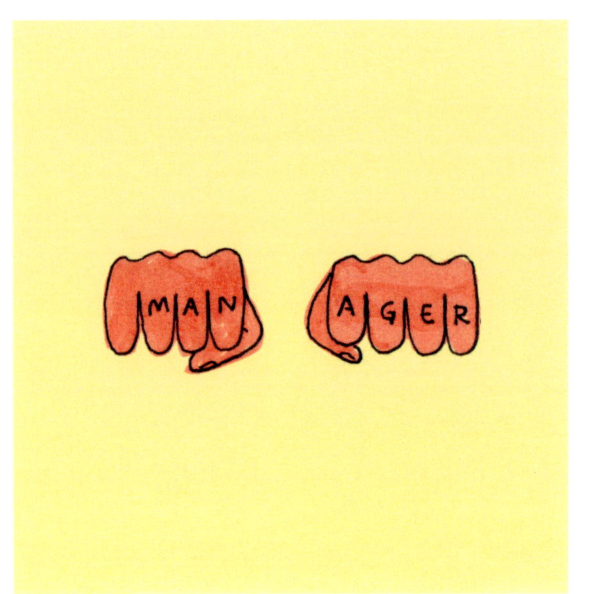

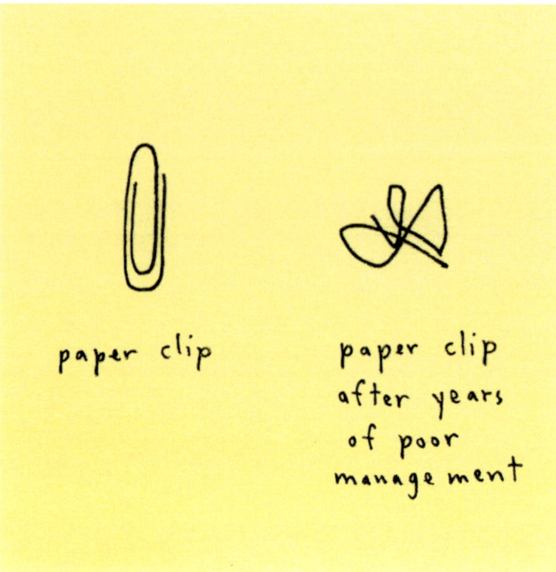

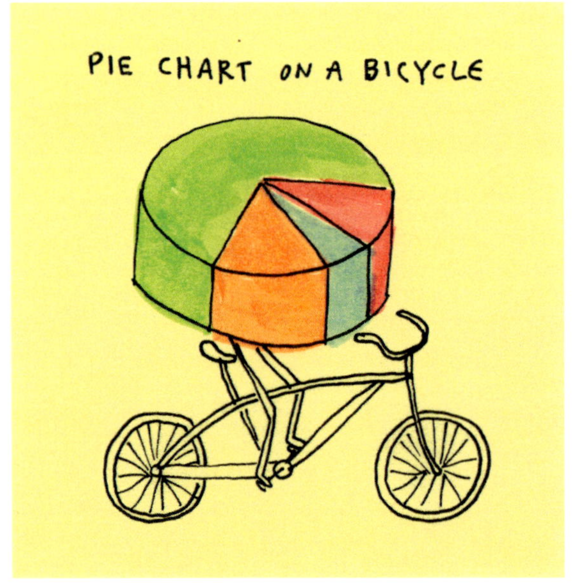

TO-DO TODAY:

MAKE BOSS HAPPY
MAKE BOSS HAPPY
MAKE BOSS HAPPY
MAKE BOSS HAPPY
MAKE BOSS HAPPY
MAKE BOSS HAPPY
DO MY JOB
MAKE BOSS HAPPY

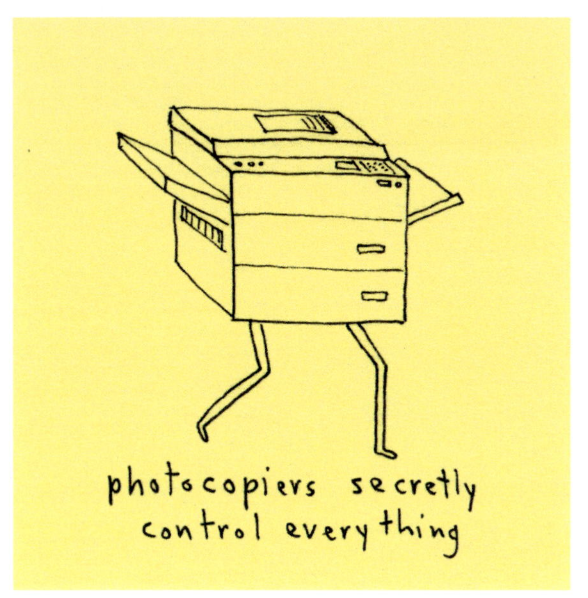
photocopiers secretly
control everything

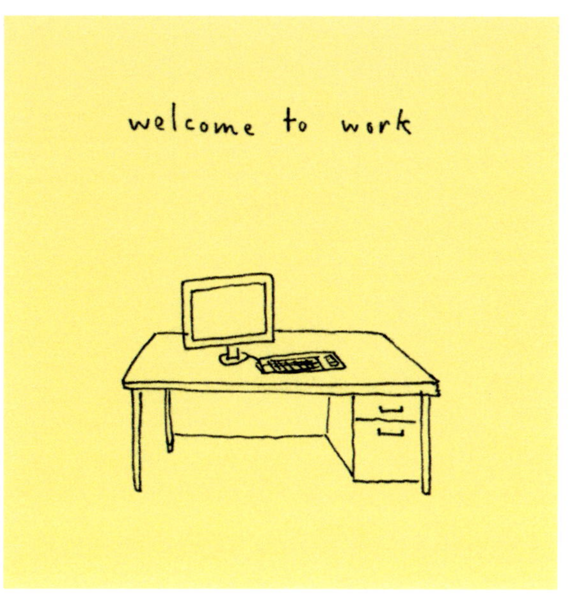
welcome to work

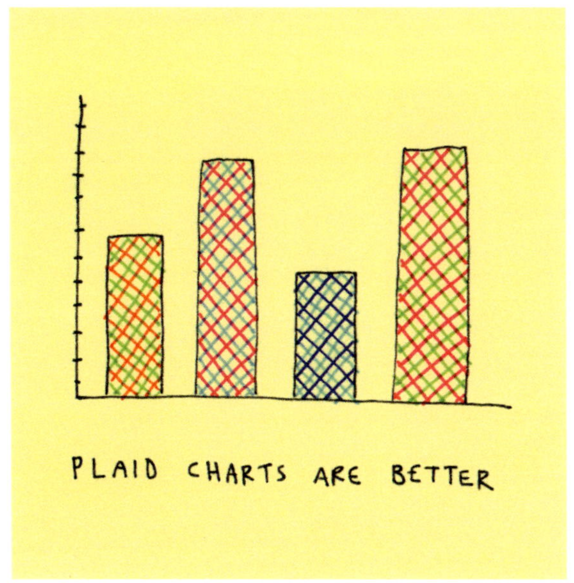
PLAID CHARTS ARE BETTER

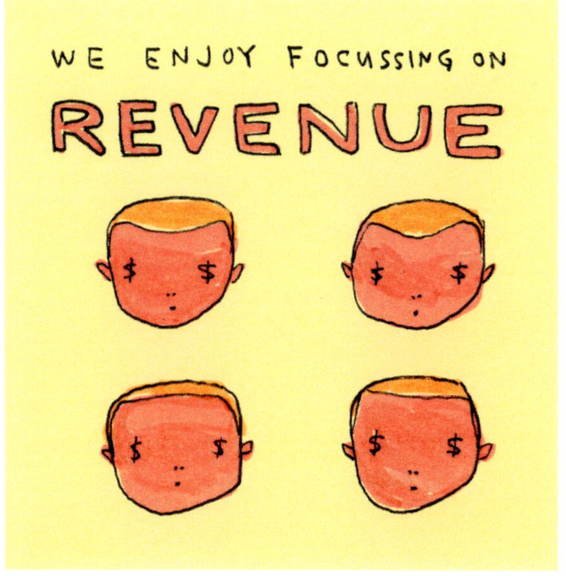
WE ENJOY FOCUSSING ON
REVENUE

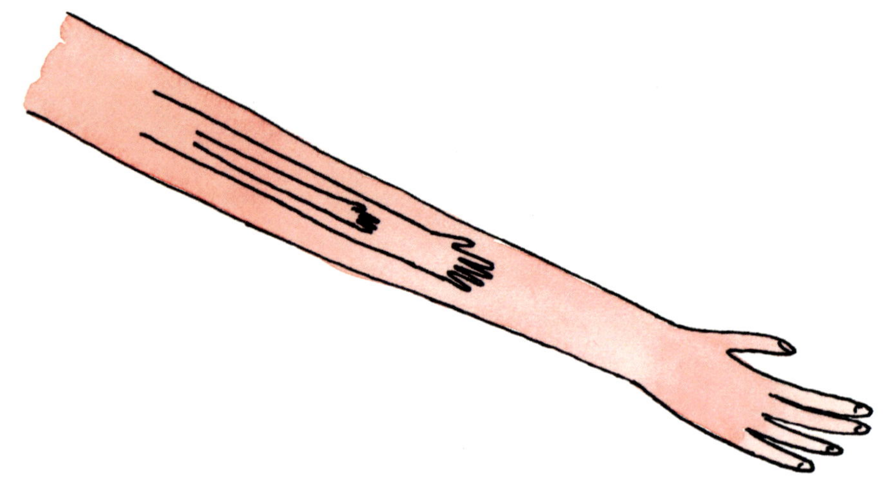

arm with a
tattoo of an arm
with a
tattoo of an arm.

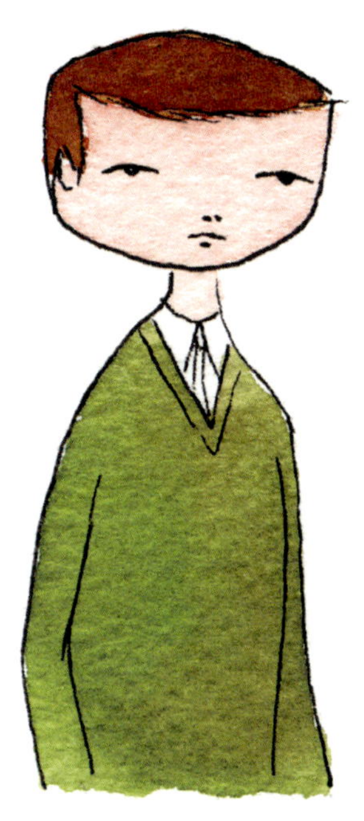

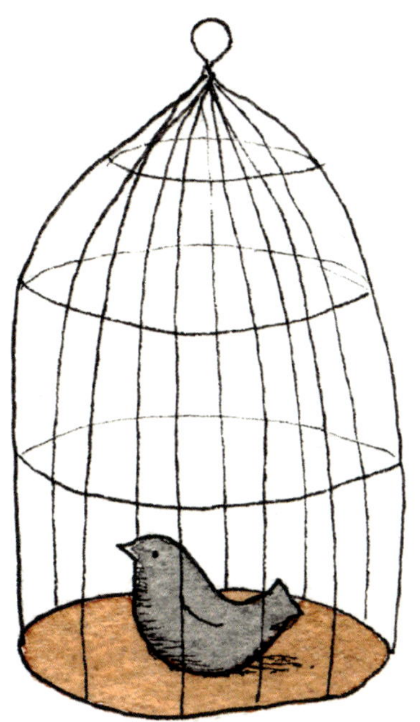

stone birds make less noise

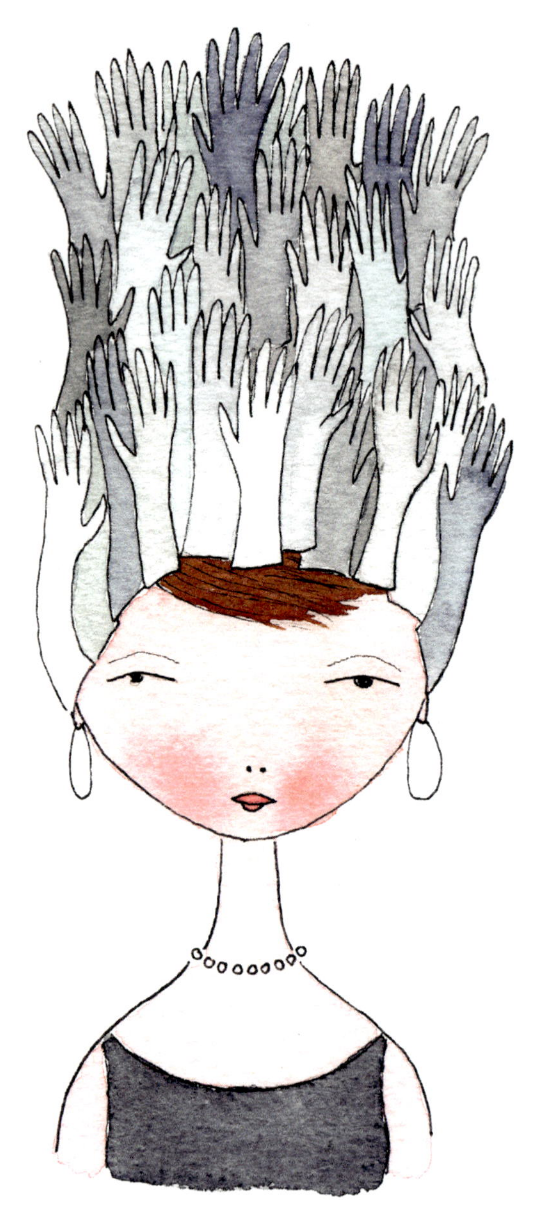

She used her collection of gloves to make the most extraordinary headdress.

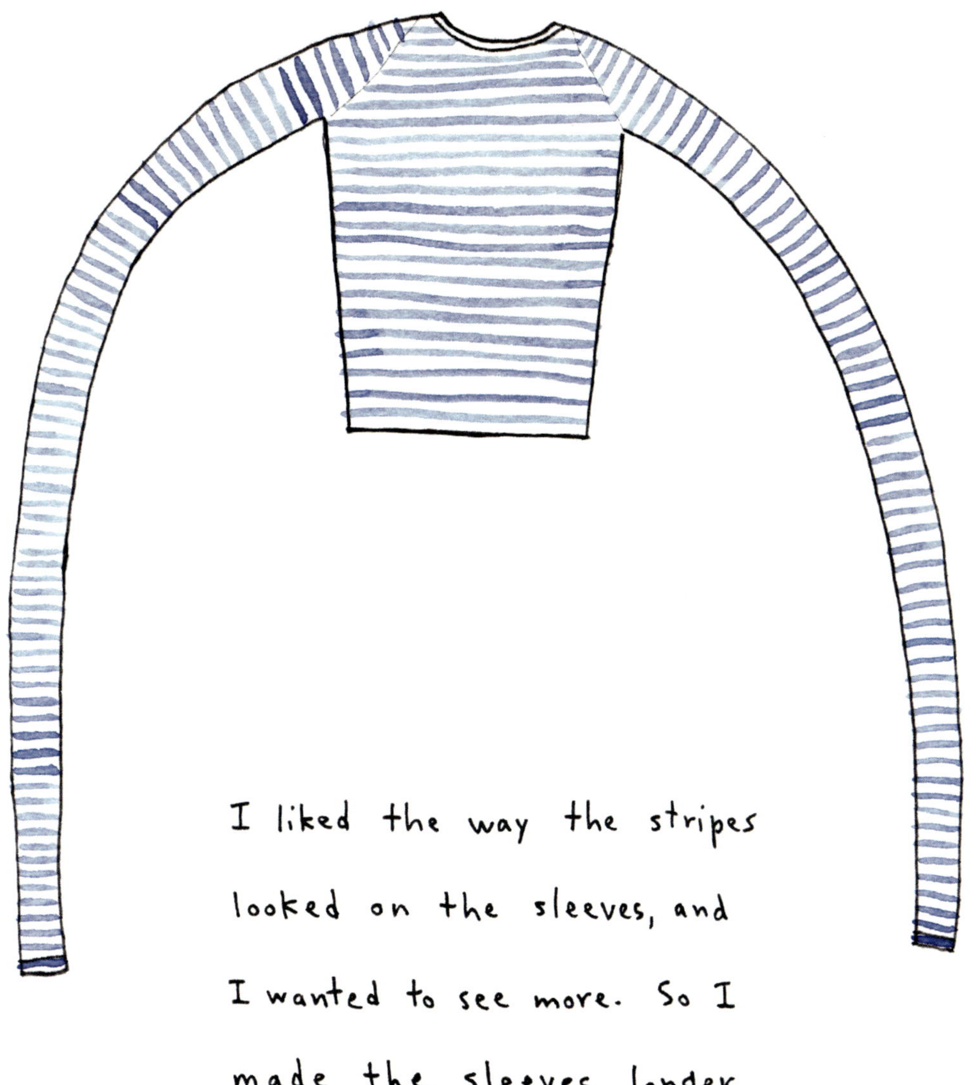

I liked the way the stripes looked on the sleeves, and I wanted to see more. So I made the sleeves longer.

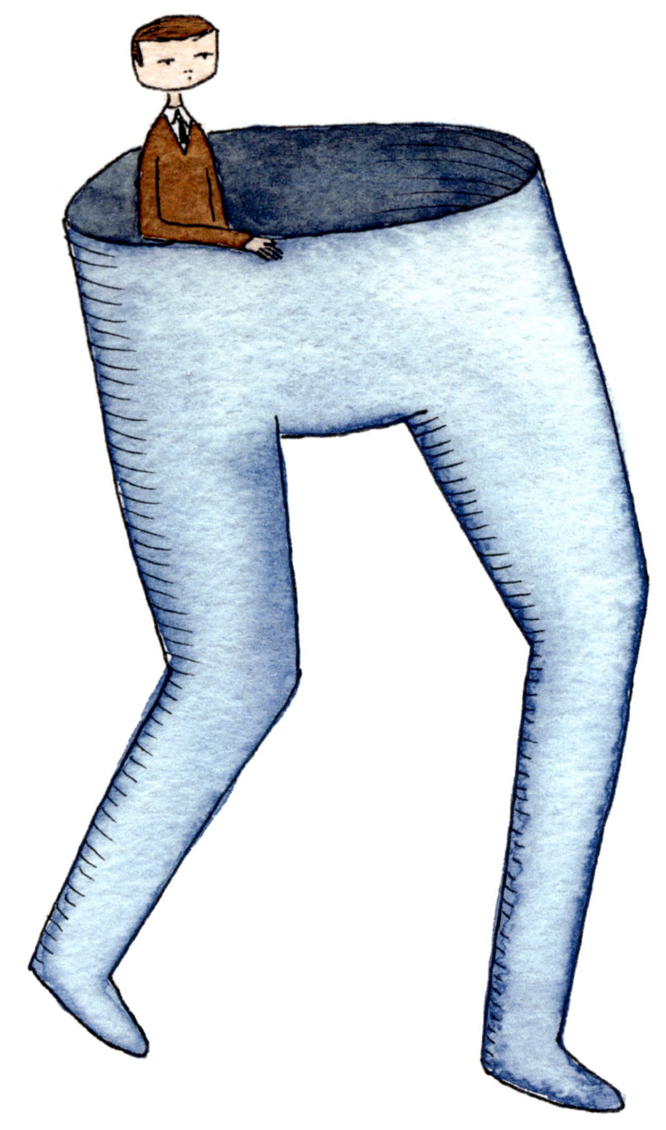

I like to get around on foot.

JUST BE

FAMOUS.

YOU'LL FEEL BETTER.

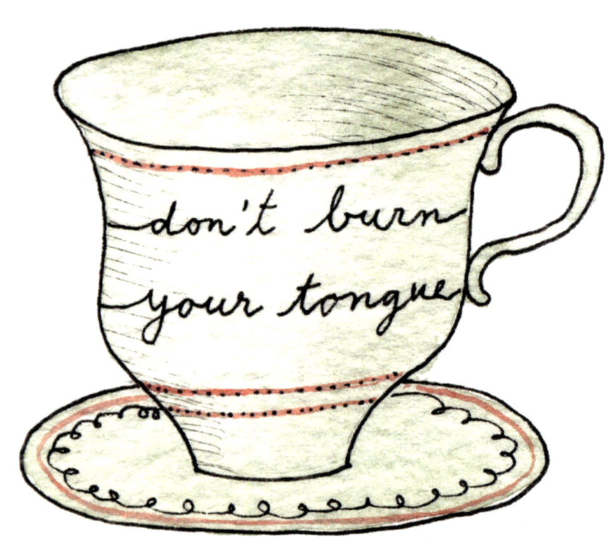
don't burn
your tongue

WHAT TO FOCUS ON:

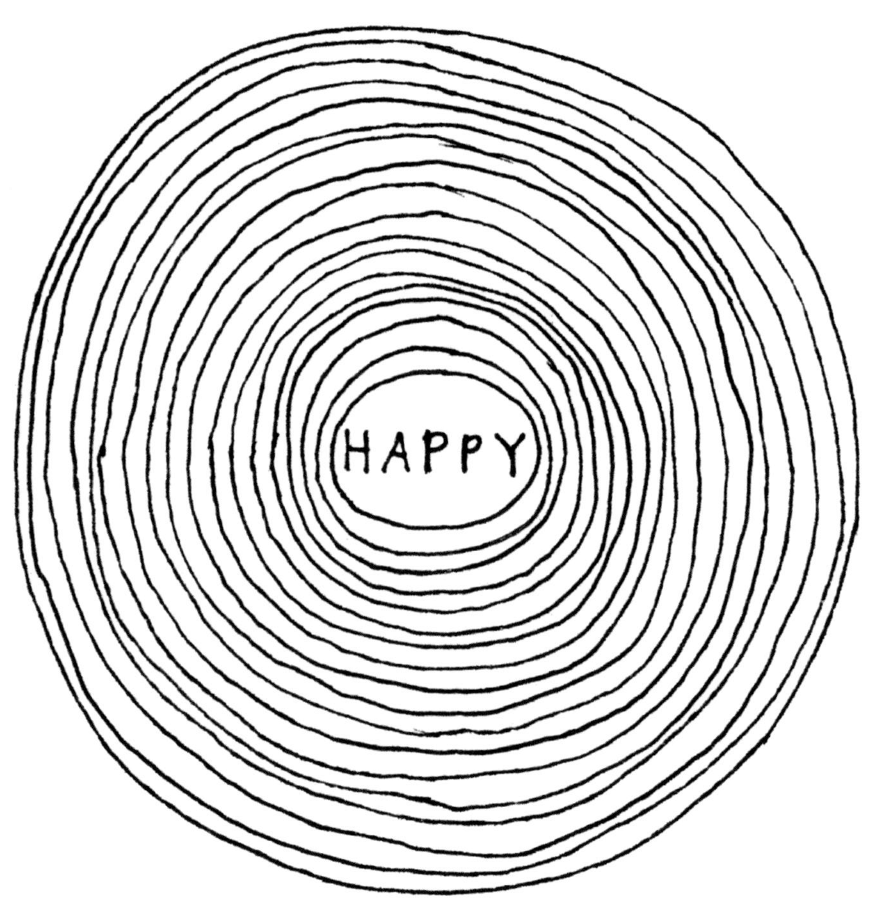

indeed

He never did very well in school, but he was particularly gifted at controlling his laser eyes.

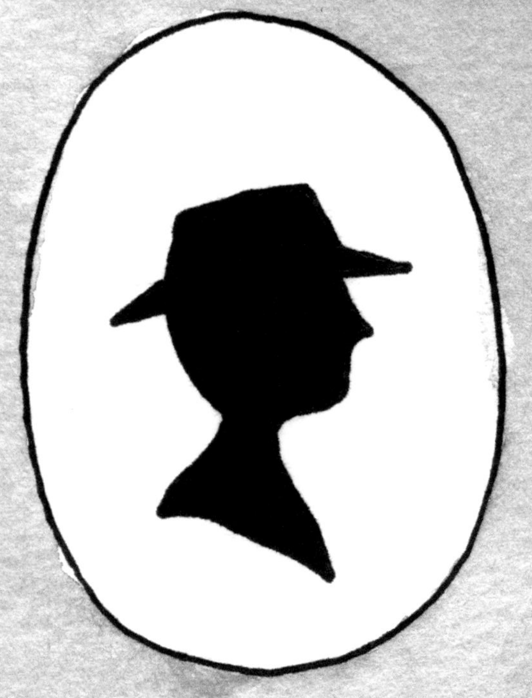

Self-portrait with a hat that's not mine

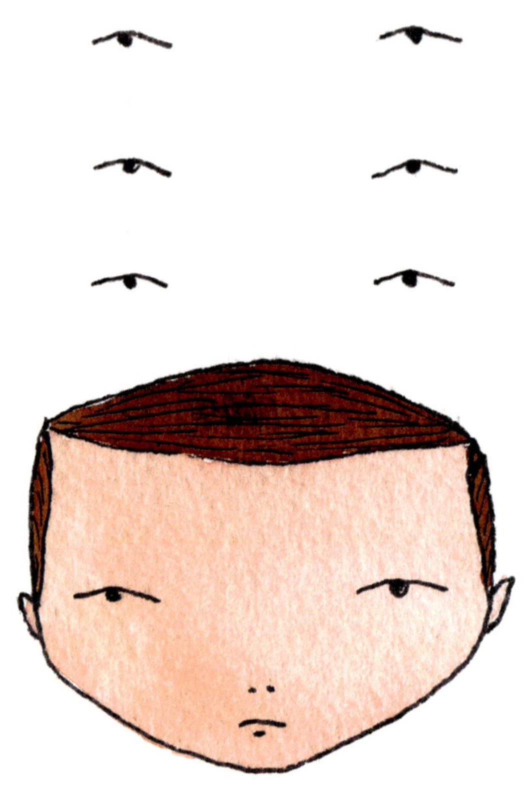

would you like some eyes?
I have extras.

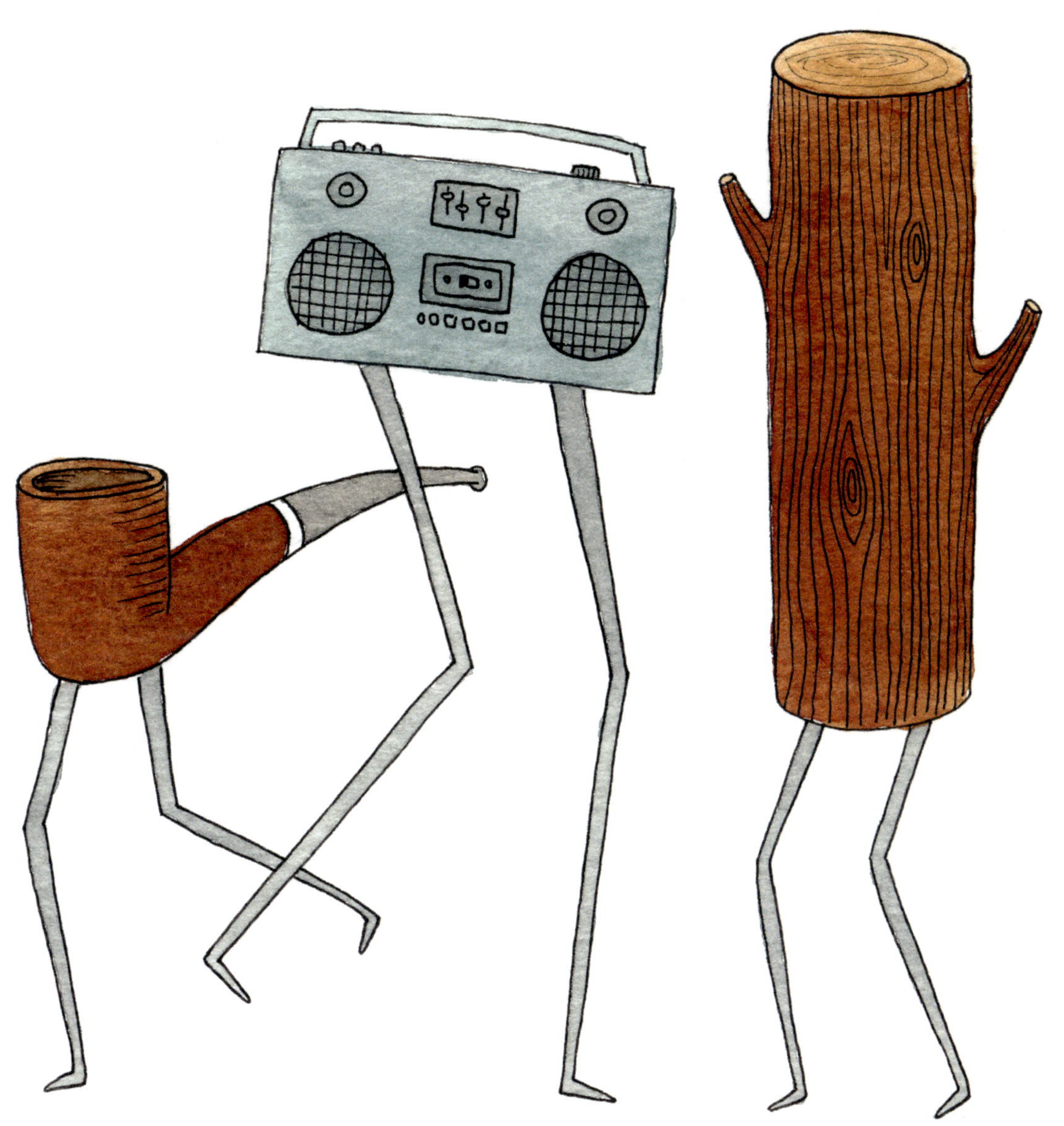

We now have legs. We shall use them to dance.

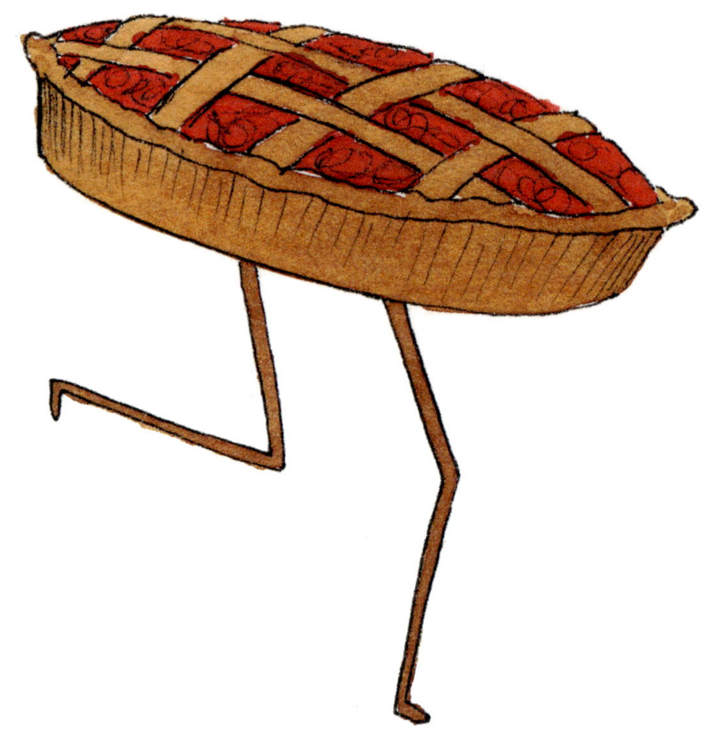

Your freshly baked pie
will cool down faster if
you let it do a little dance.

wear these oven mitts

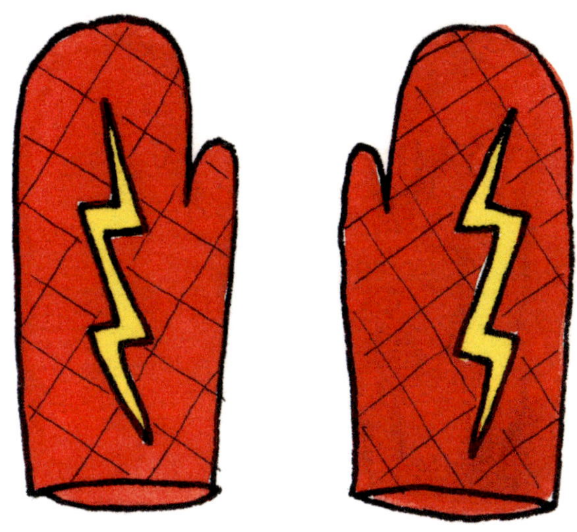

cook with awesomeness

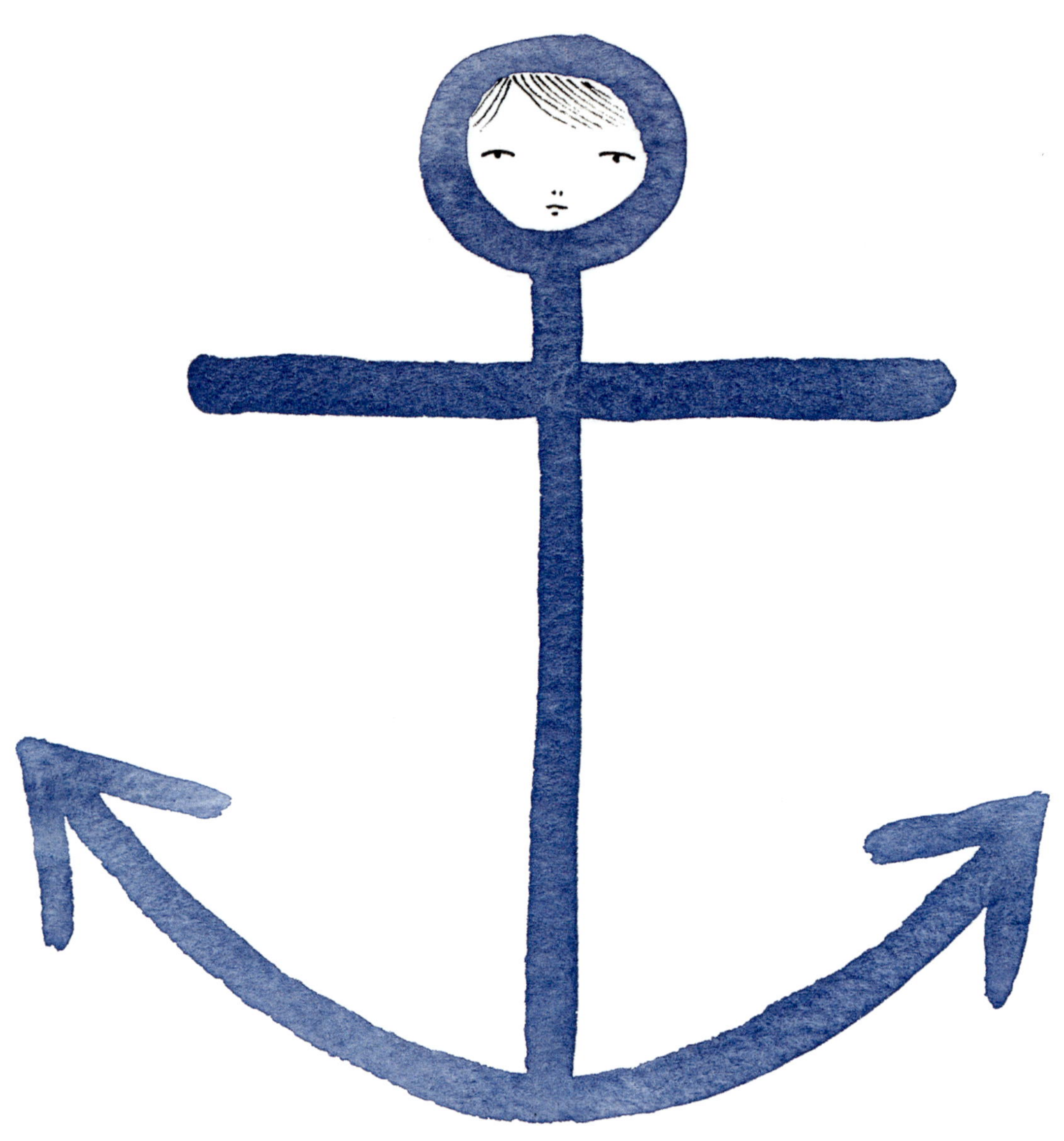

you anchor me

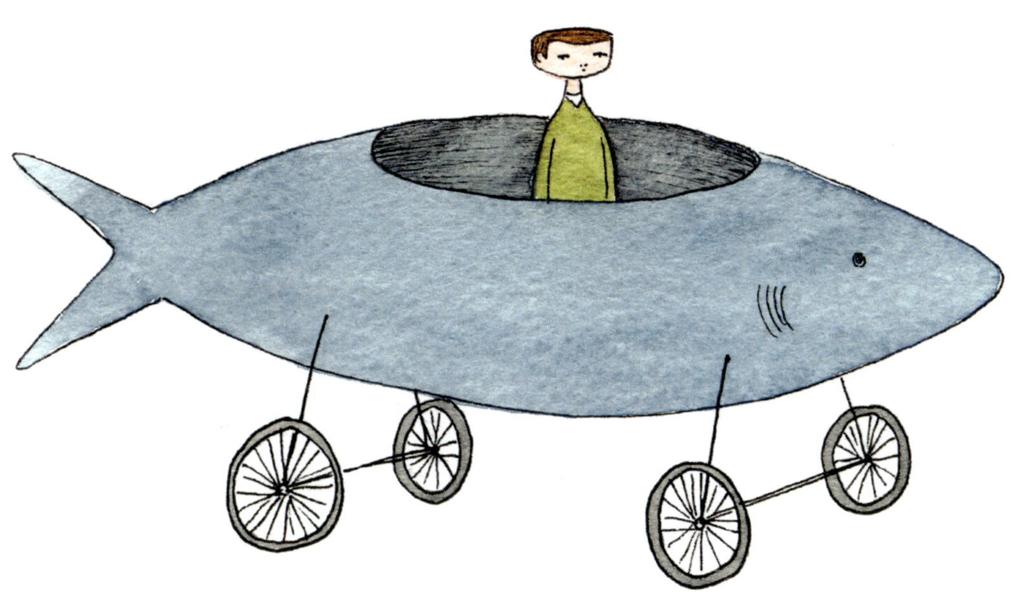

An unnecessary combination

if you were a chair,
and you were tired,
you would do this:

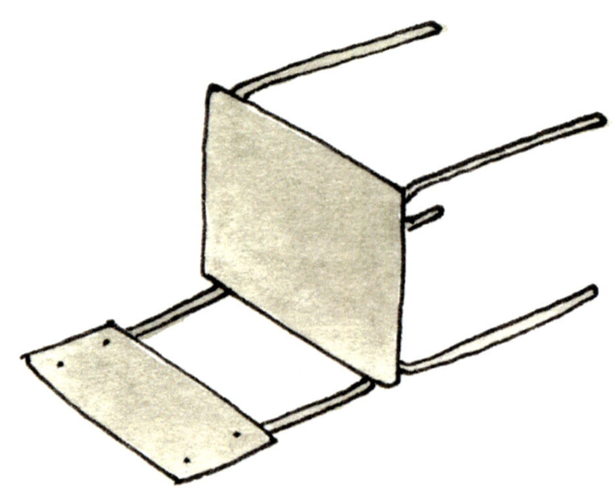

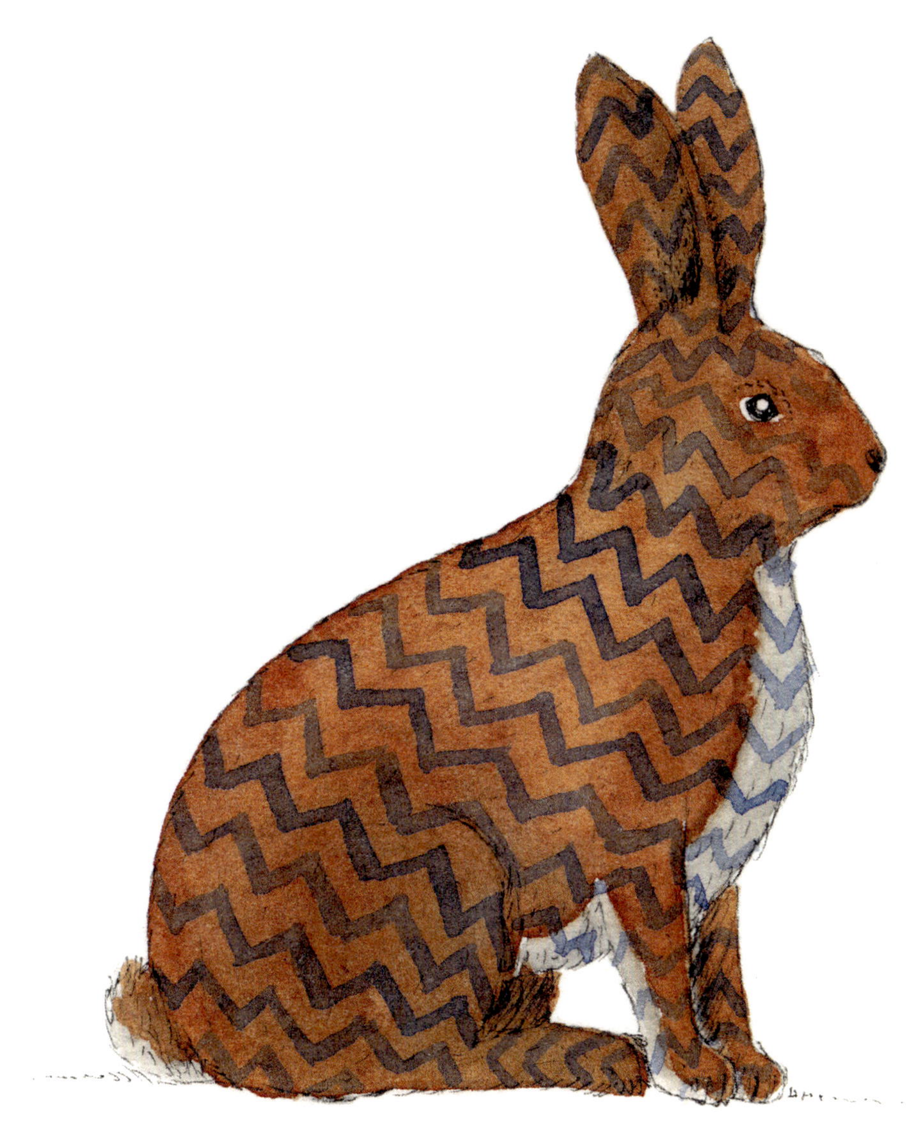

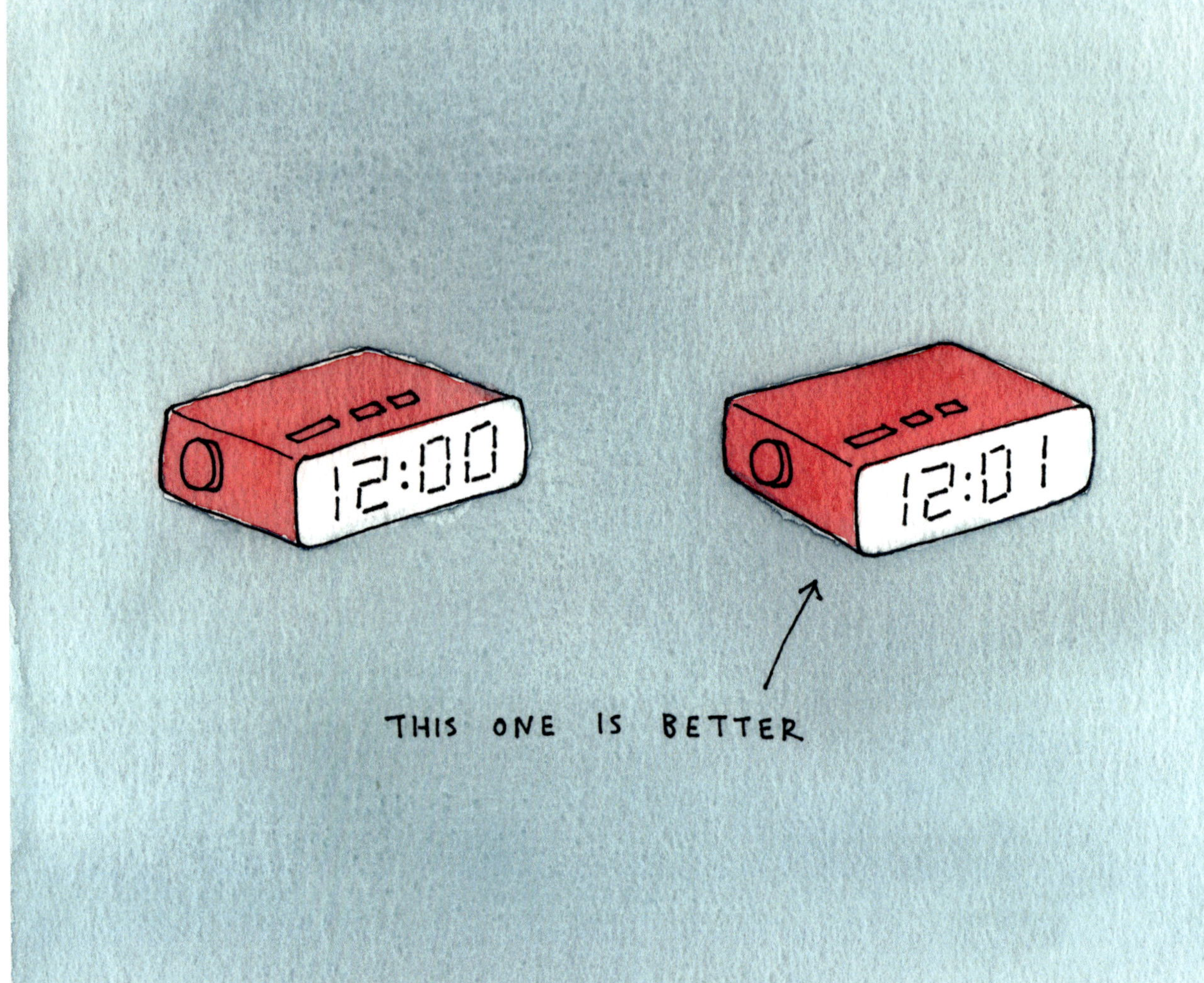
12:00
12:01
THIS ONE IS BETTER

THIS BRAND OF PLAID SHIRTS

MAKES US FEEL OUTDOORSY

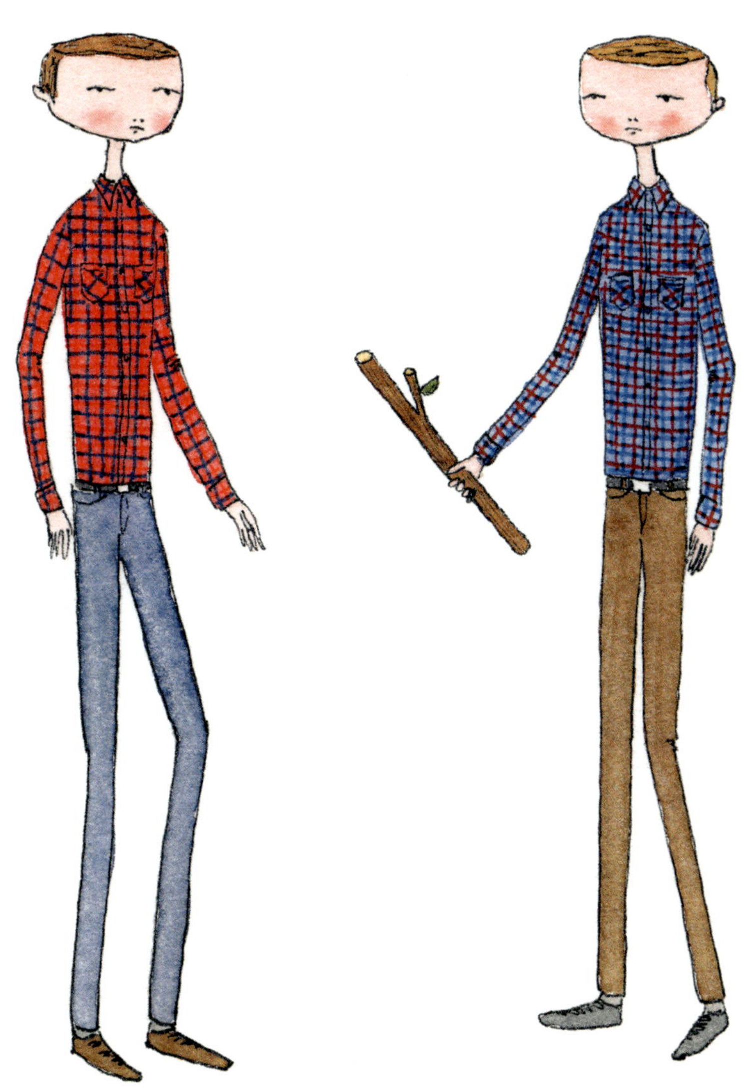

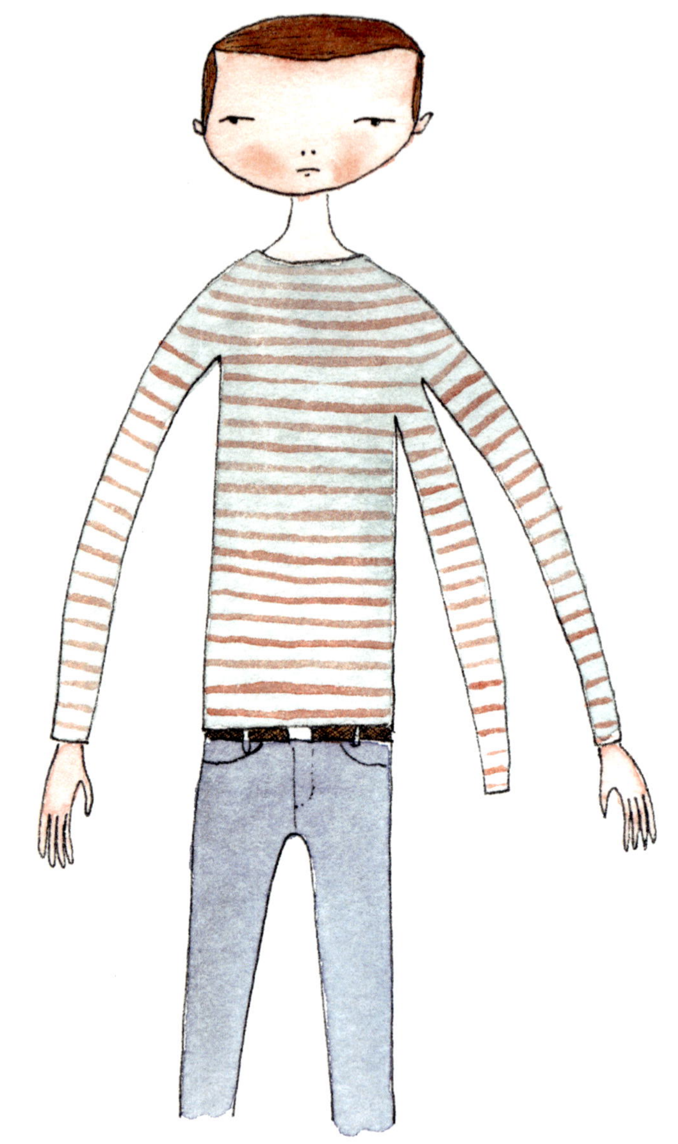

Of course, he only has two arms,

but three-armed shirts were on sale.

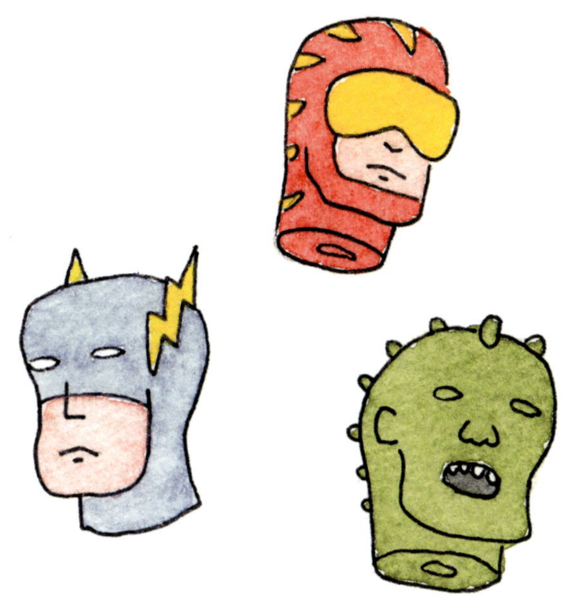

severed heads
of action figures

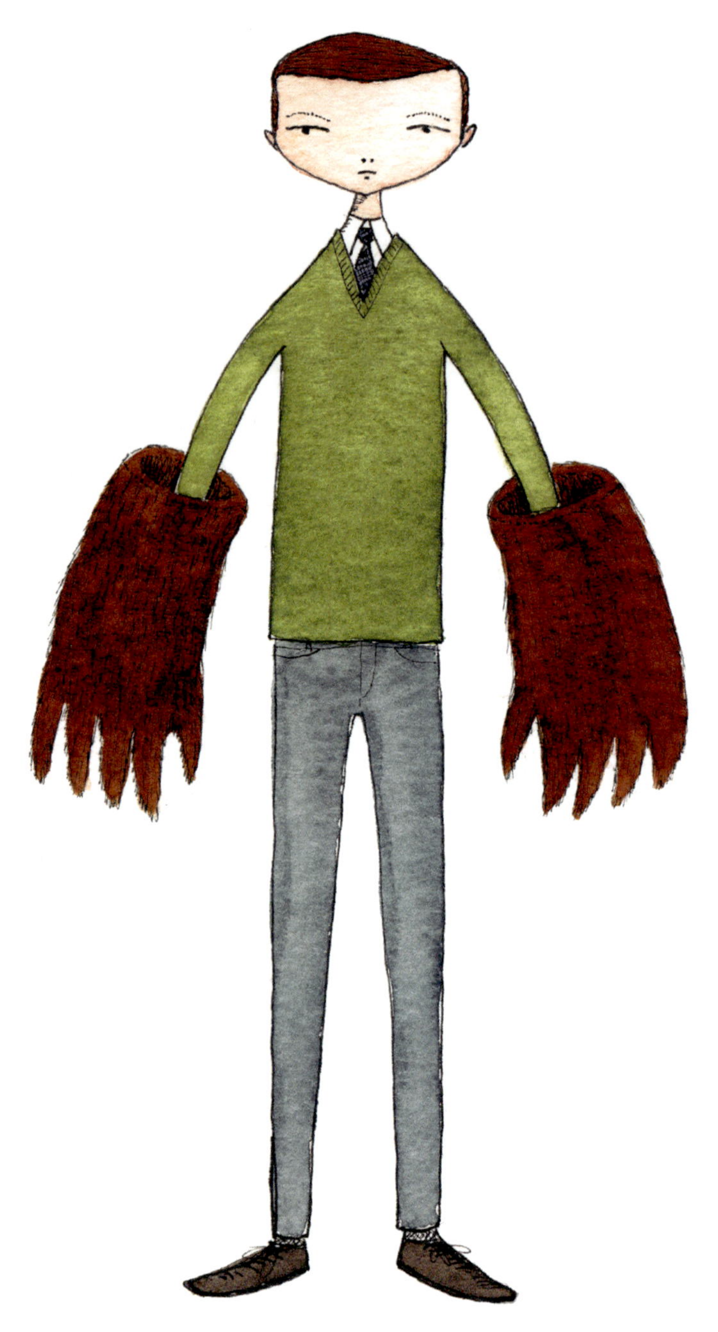

Wearing his giant yeti gloves
gave him a boost of confidence.

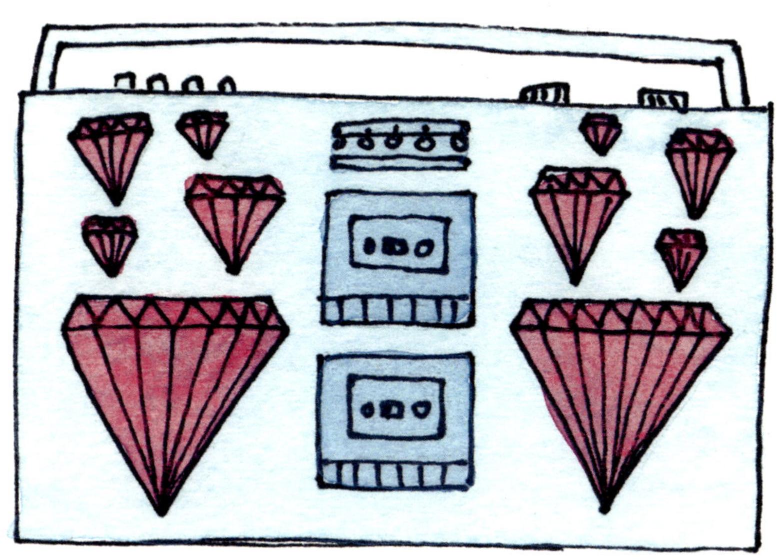

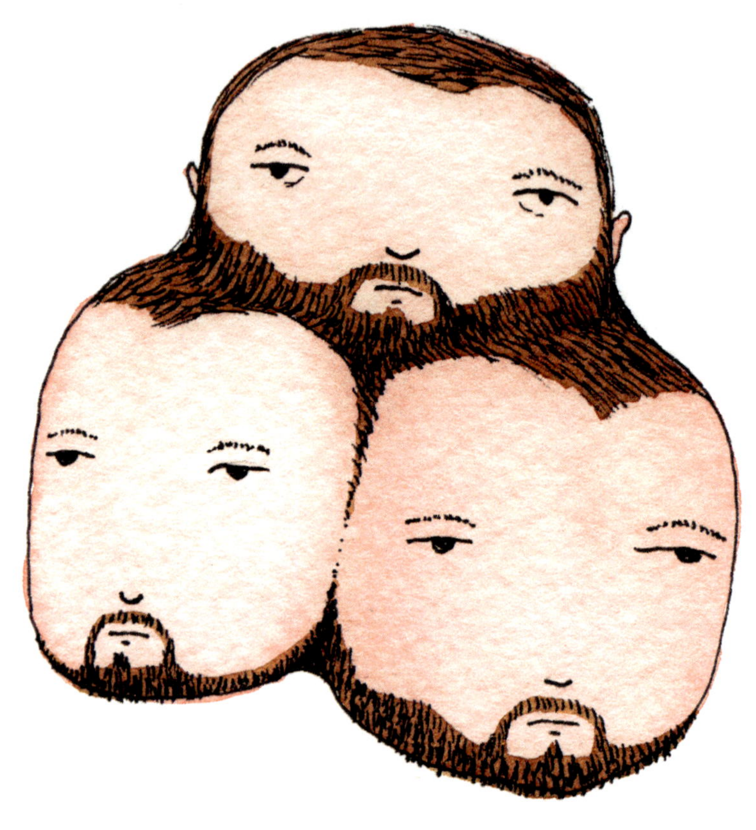

we always work much better

when we put our heads together

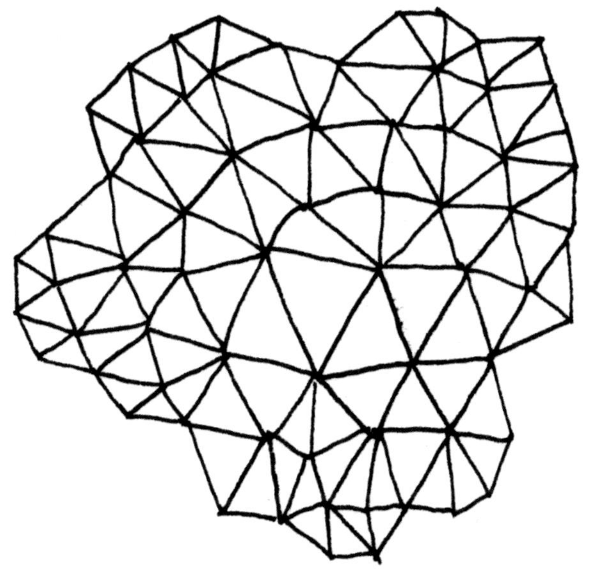

GOD MADE ME DRAW THIS

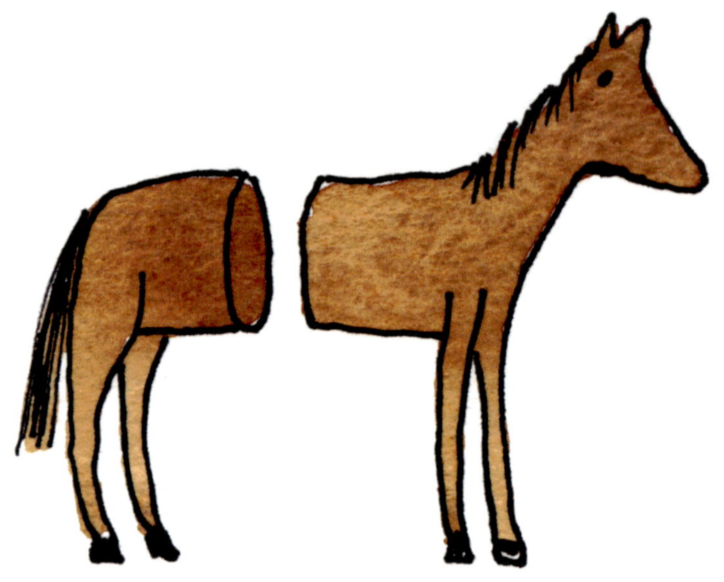

You are less likely to notice that I can't draw a horse very well if I cut it in half.

I have a crush on TREES

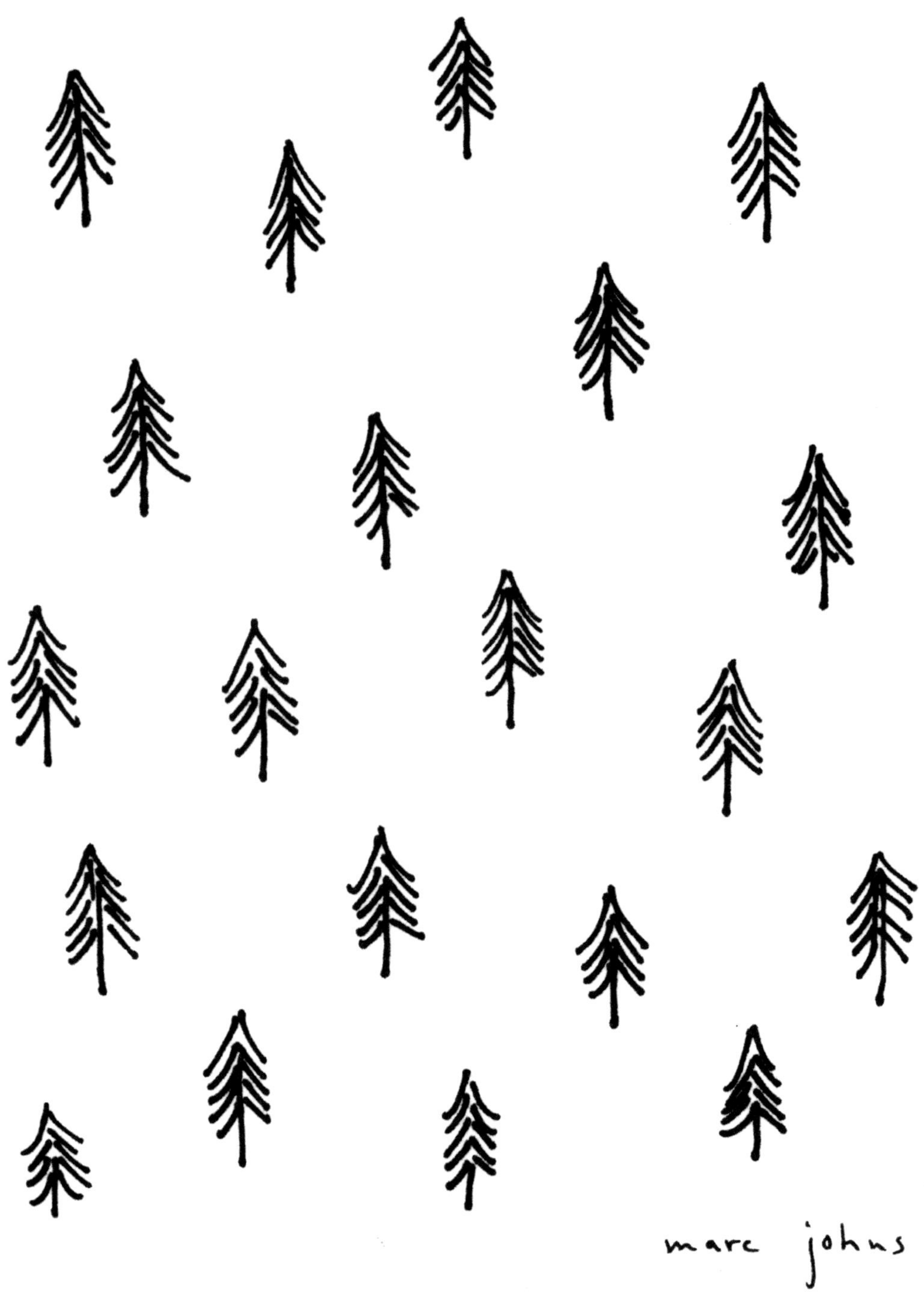

LET'S FOCUS ON THE UNATTAINABLE

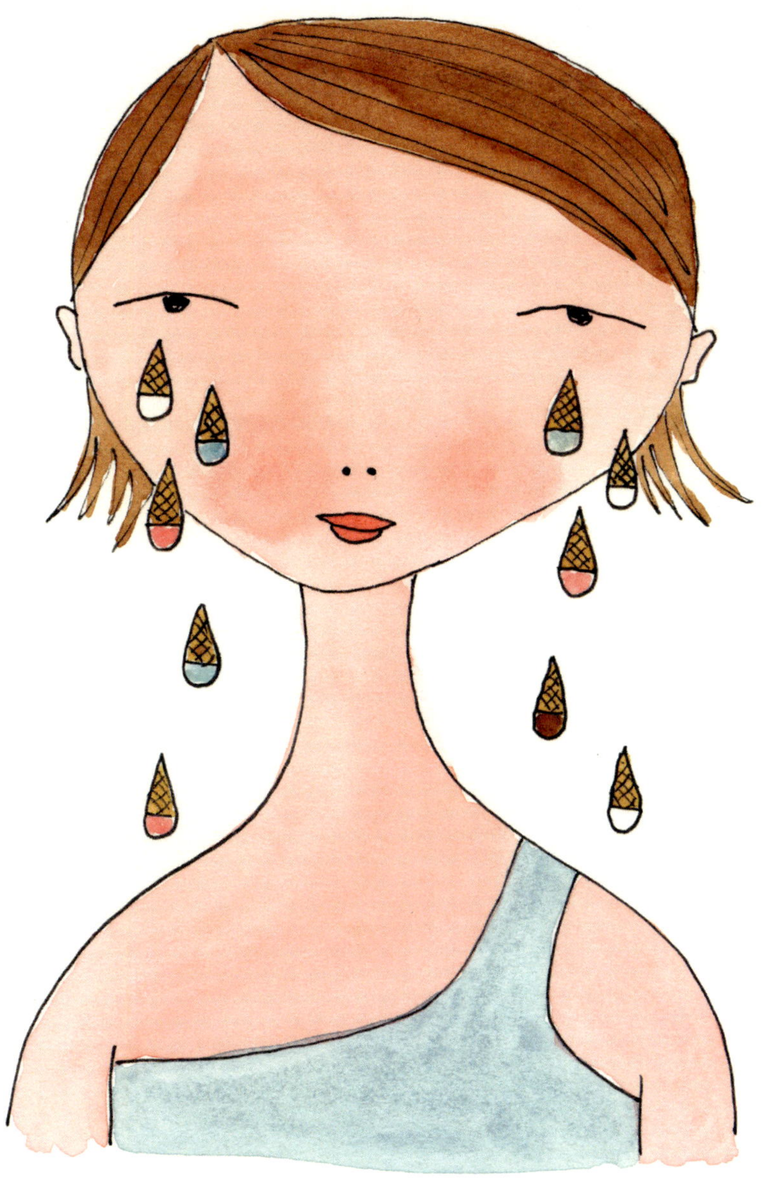

ice cream cone tears are more delicious

RAINBOW TYPES

regular

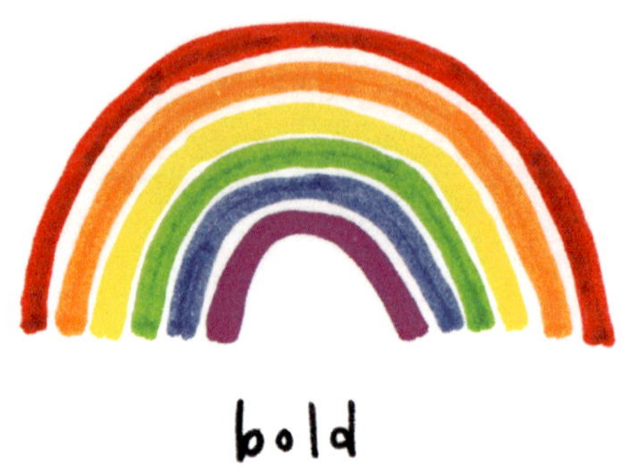

bold

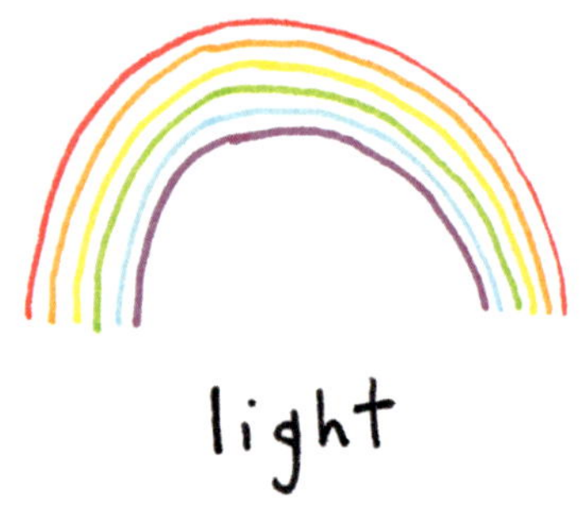

light

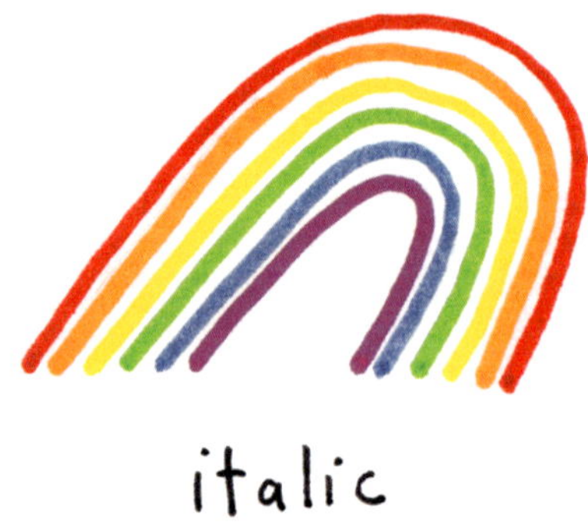

italic

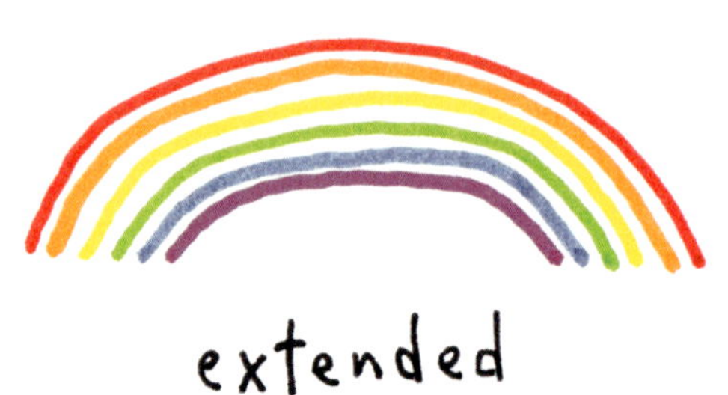

extended

condensed

The spherical bear
just wasn't aware;
his abnormal condition
never dampened his mission.

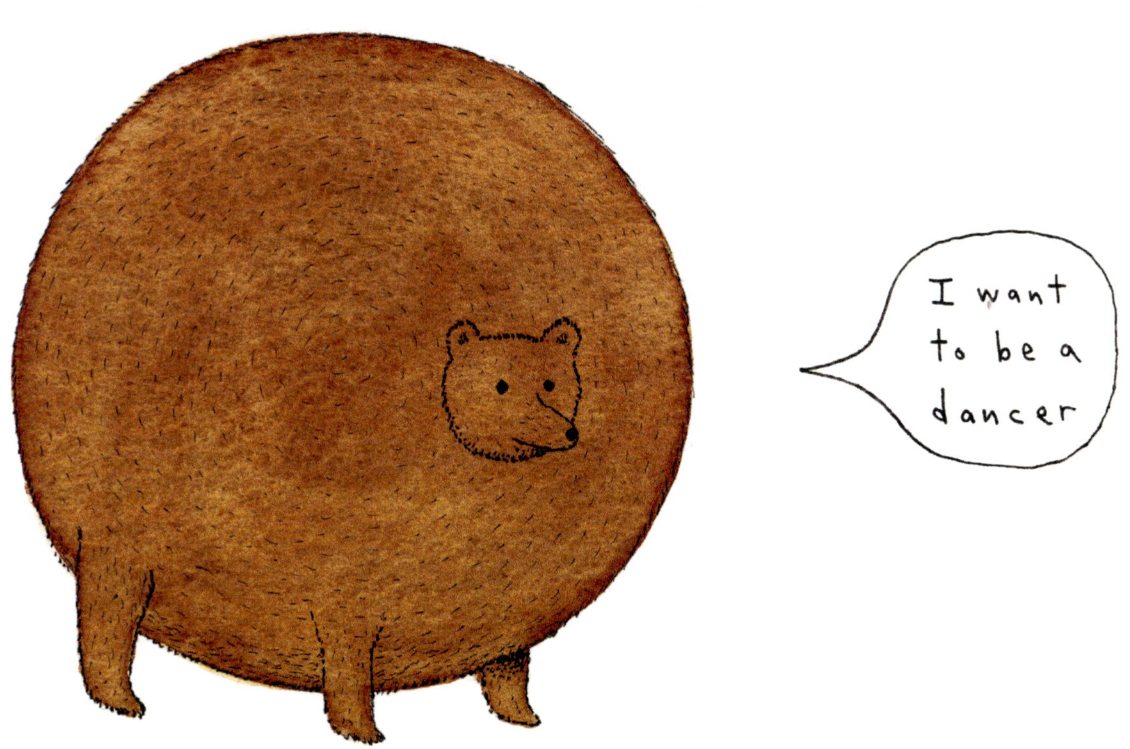

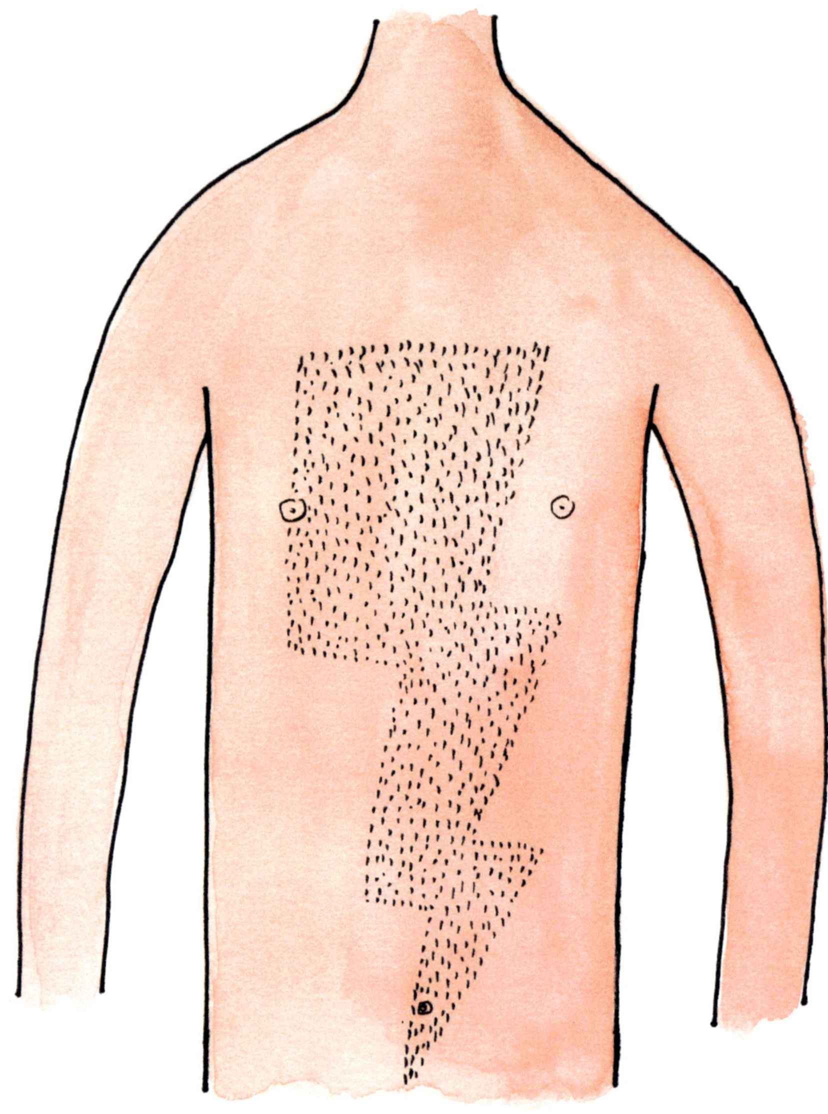

a new trend in chest hair

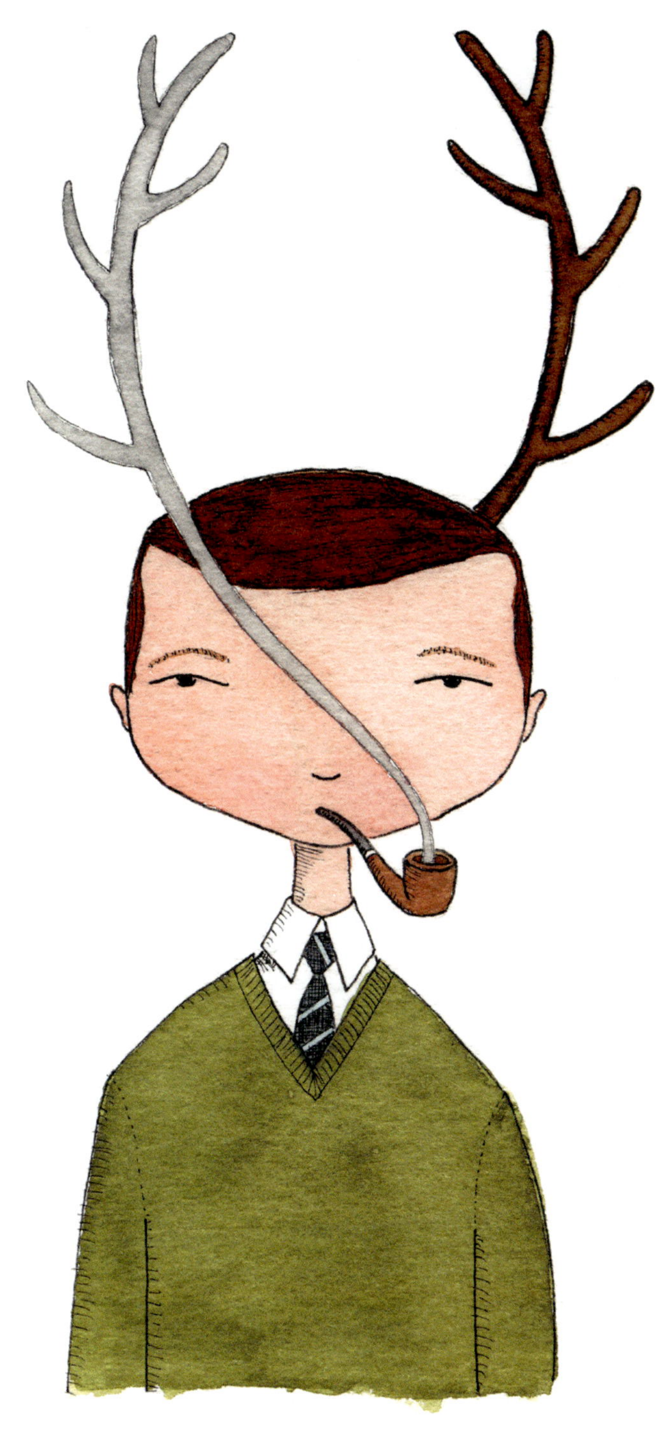

one real antler, one imagined.

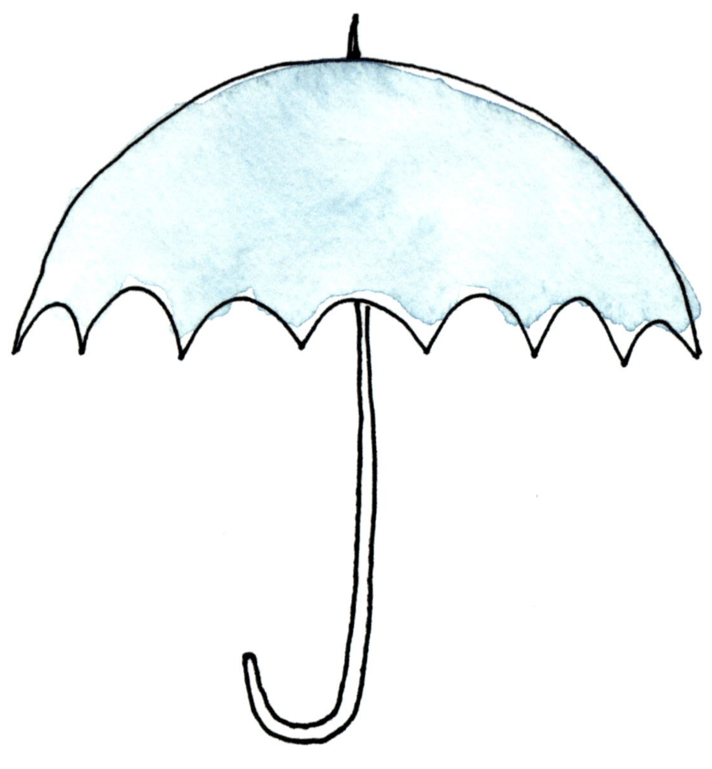

this drawing of an umbrella
will not keep you dry.

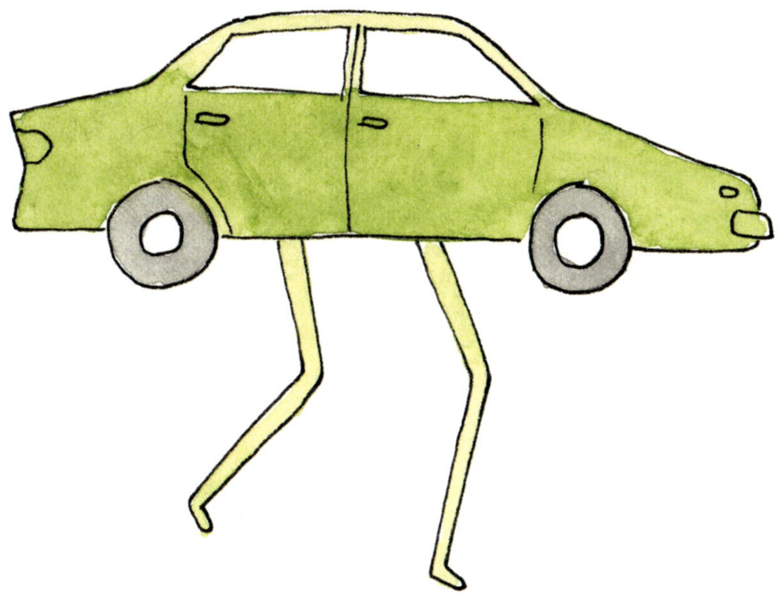

too drunk to drive,
the four-door sedan
walked home.

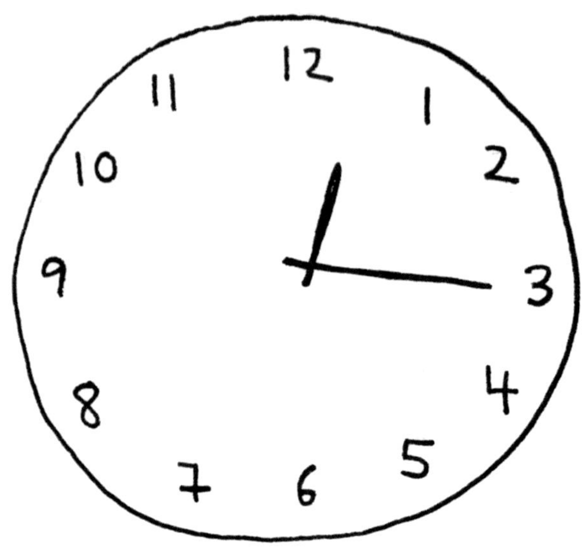

TICK FUCKING TOCK
FUCKING TICK FUCKING
TOCK FUCKING TICK
FUCKING TOCK

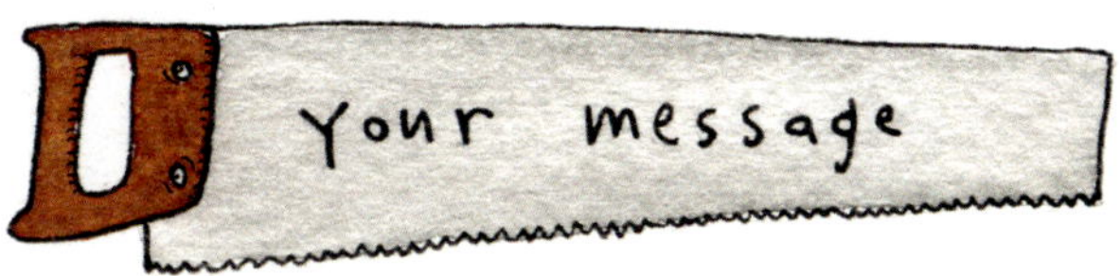
your message

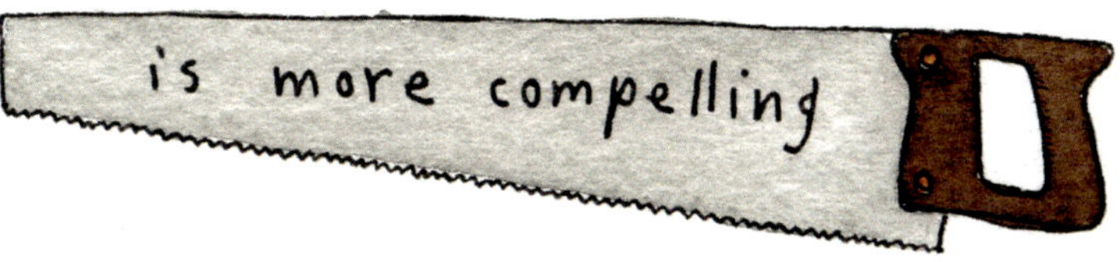
is more compelling

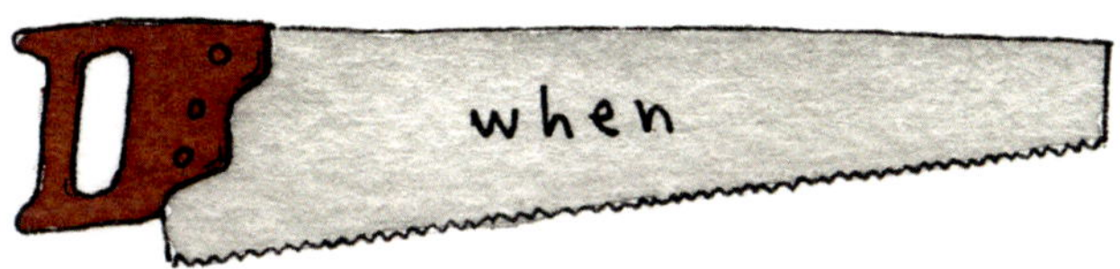
when

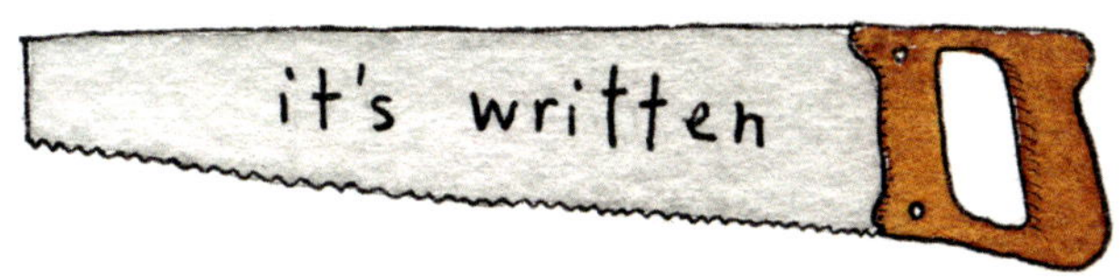
it's written

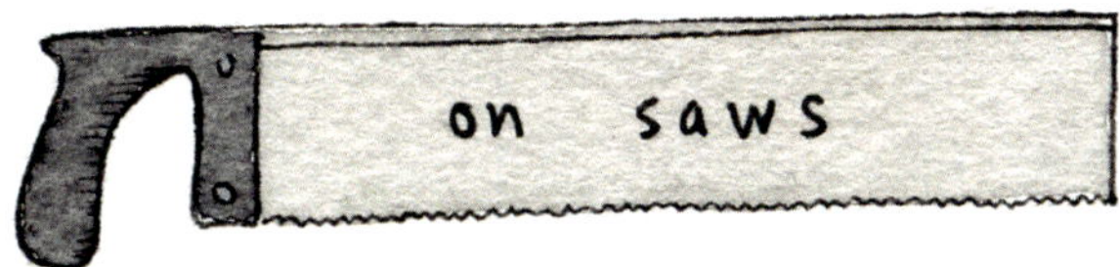
on saws

this is a stick.

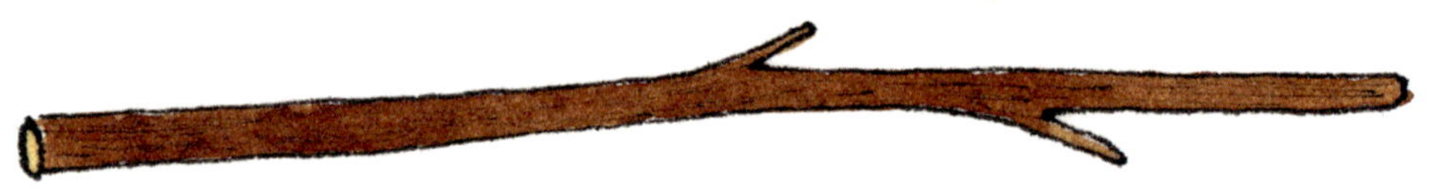

use it to conduct an orchestra.

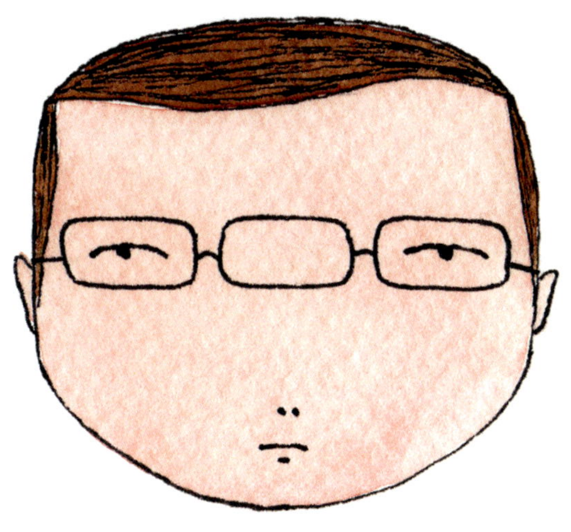

no one could see
his third eye, but
he knew it was there.

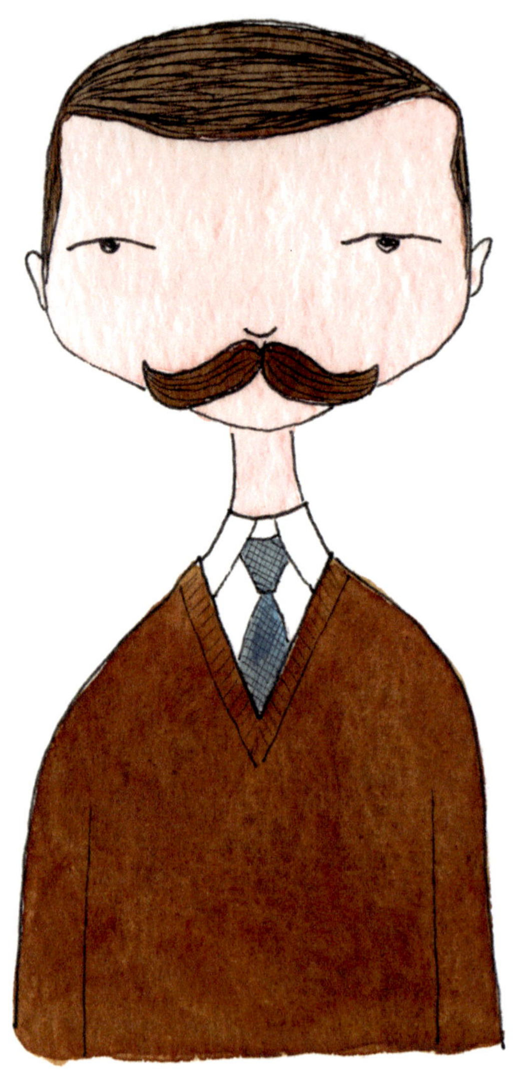

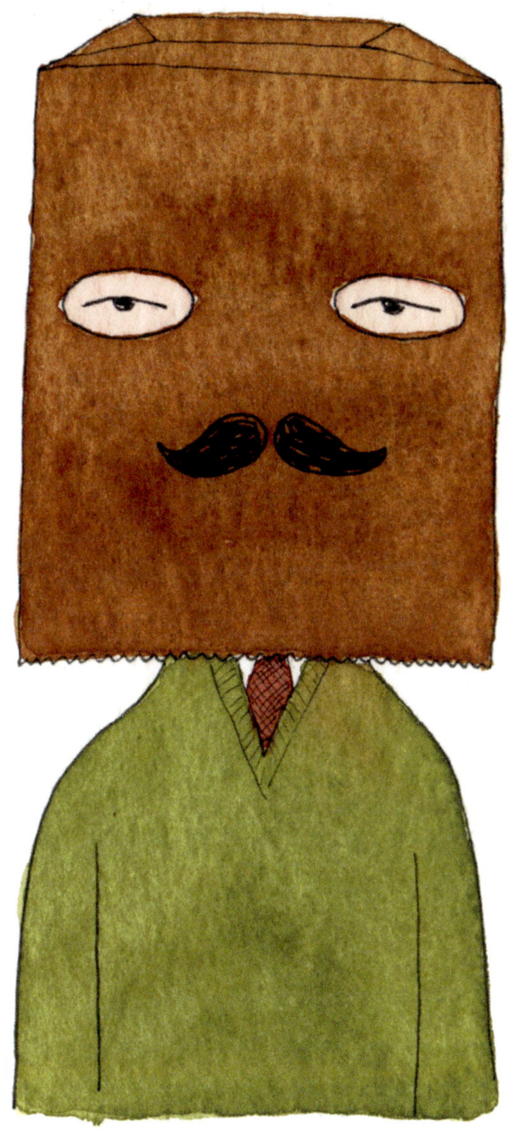

Orange reading David Foster Wallace

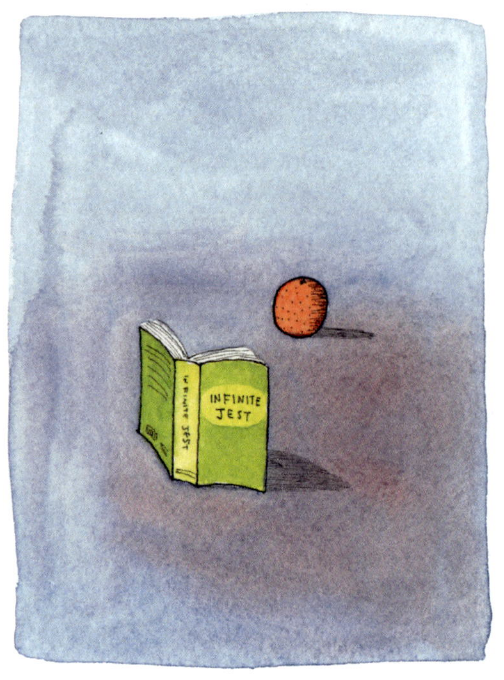

Ruler reading Oscar Wilde

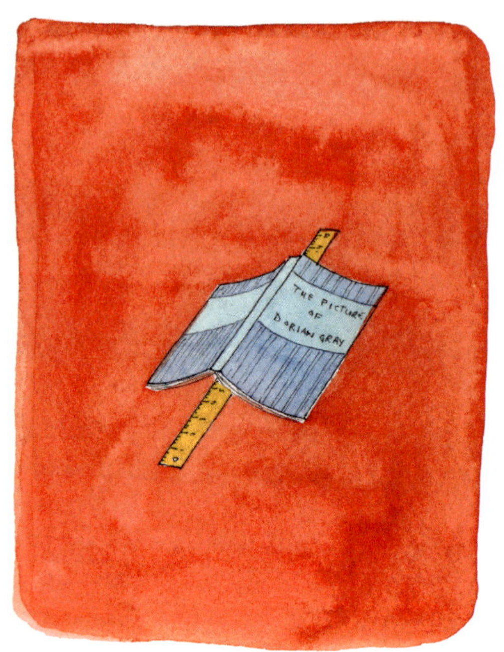

Chair reading Jane Austen

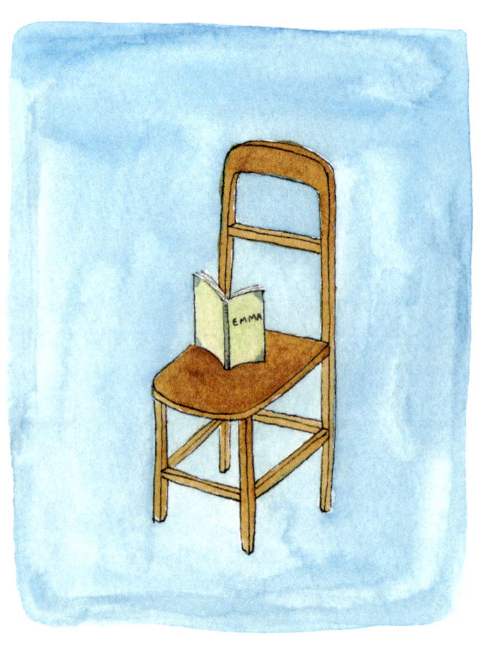

Electrical outlet reading Proust

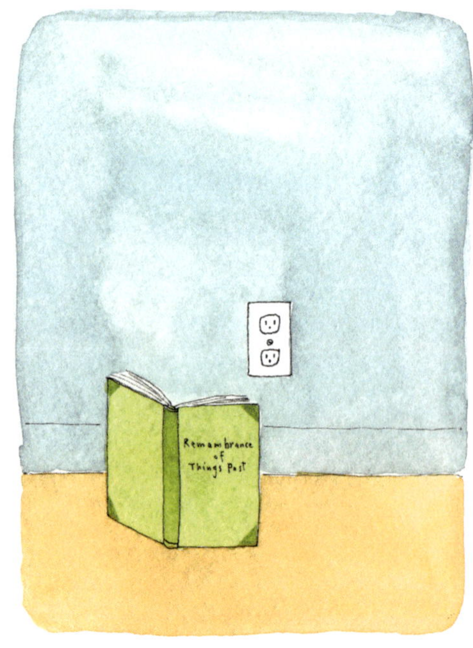

Bananas reading Shakespeare

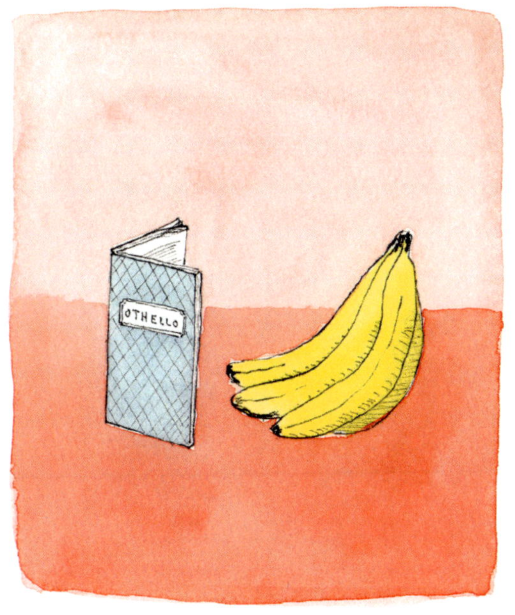

Globe reading Henry David Thoreau

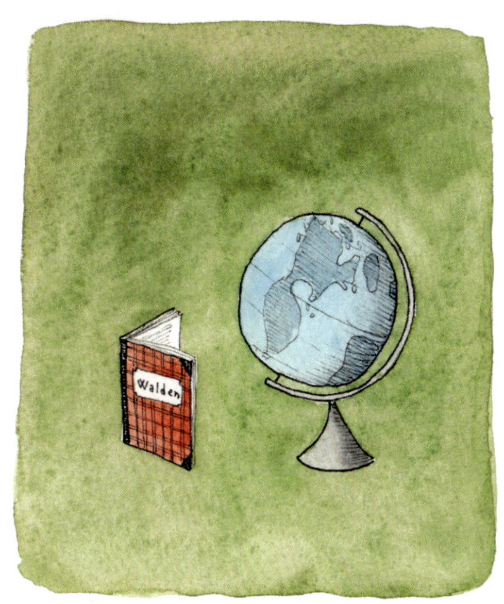

Frying pan reading Walt Whitman

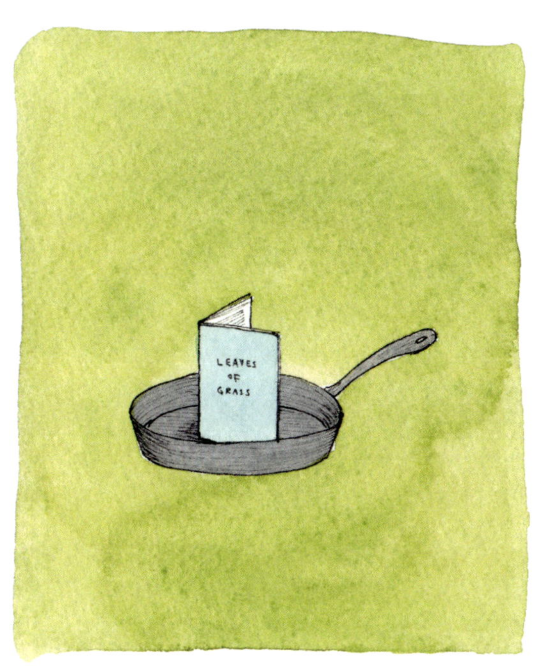

Salt shaker reading J.D. Salinger

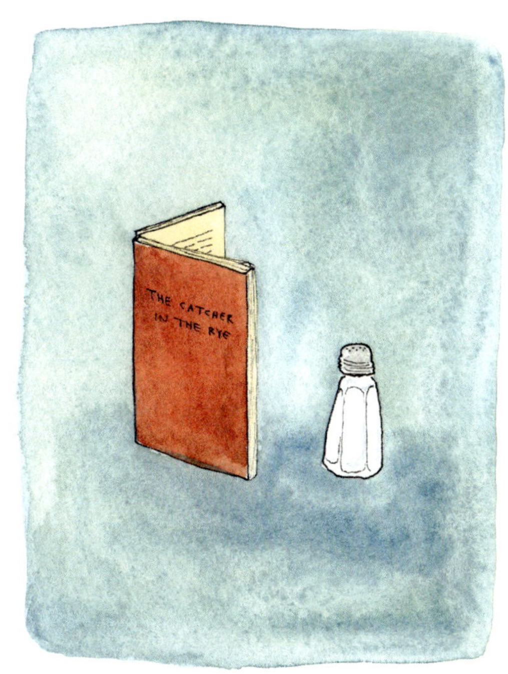

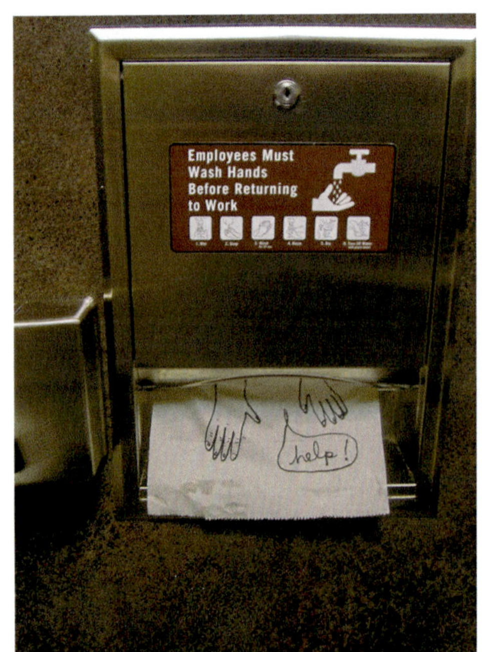
Employees Must
Wash Hands
Before Returning
to Work
help!

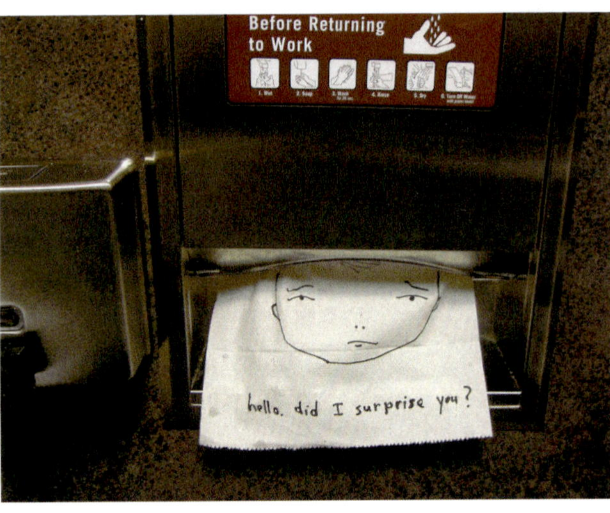
Before Returning
to Work
hello. did I surprise you?

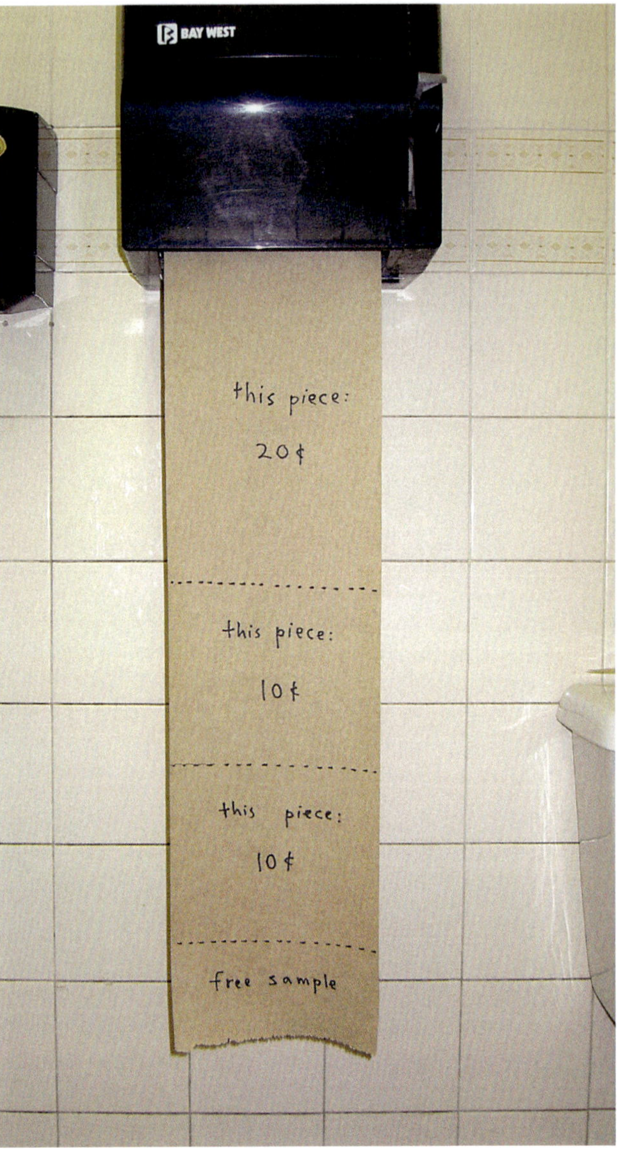
BAY WEST
this piece:
20¢
this piece:
10¢
this piece:
10¢
free sample

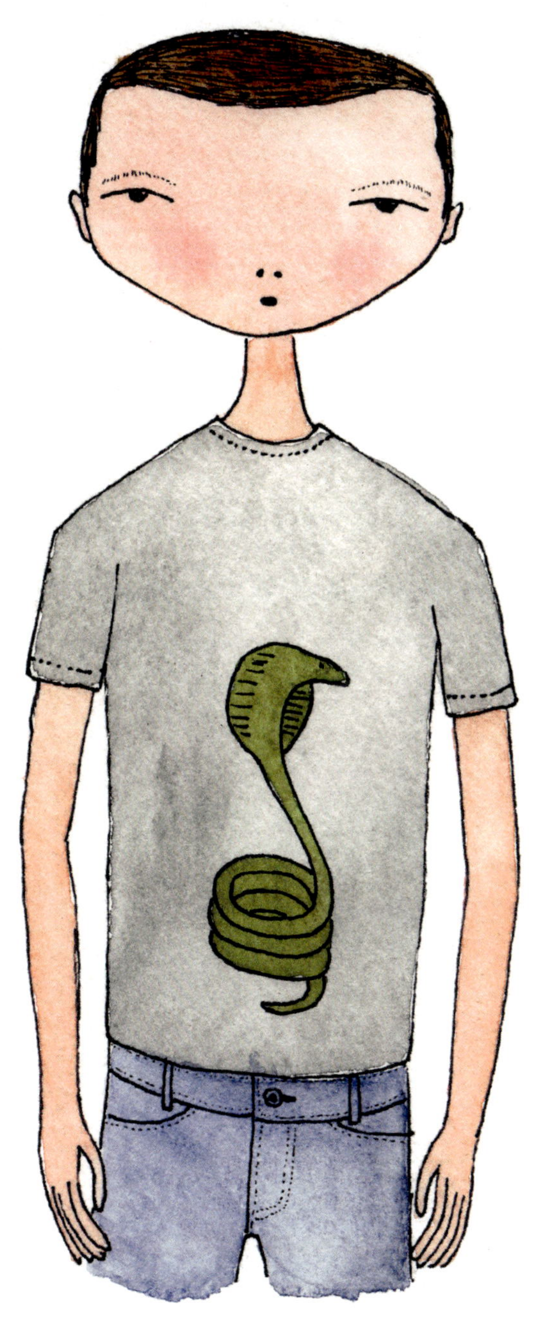

He has a cobra t-shirt.
He is therefore dangerous.

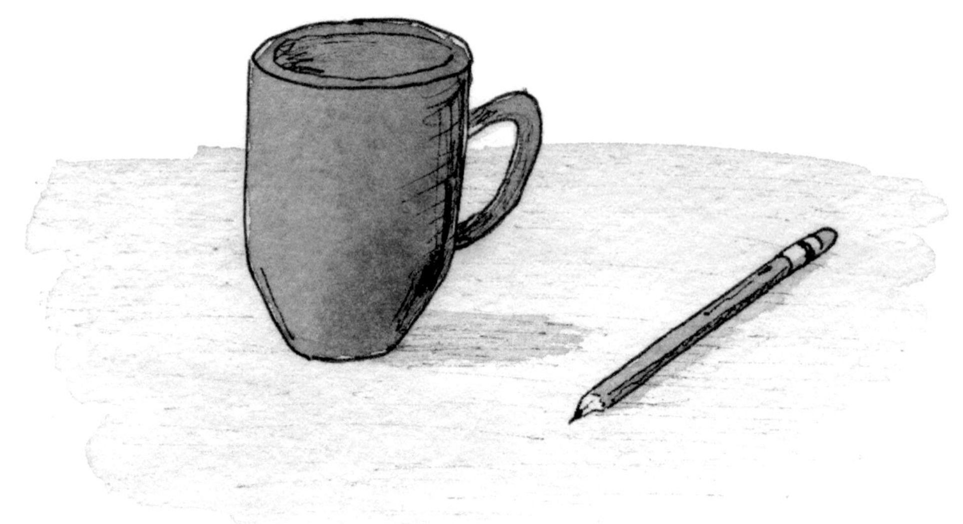

I made this drawing while I was waiting for my computer to save a file but it took so long I figured it was stuck so I just rebooted it, which meant I lost the file, but now I have this drawing.

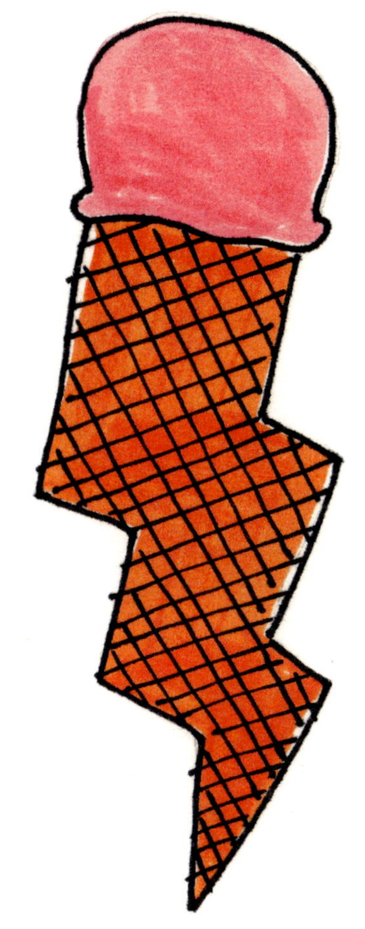

let's make ice cream cones shaped like lightning bolts.

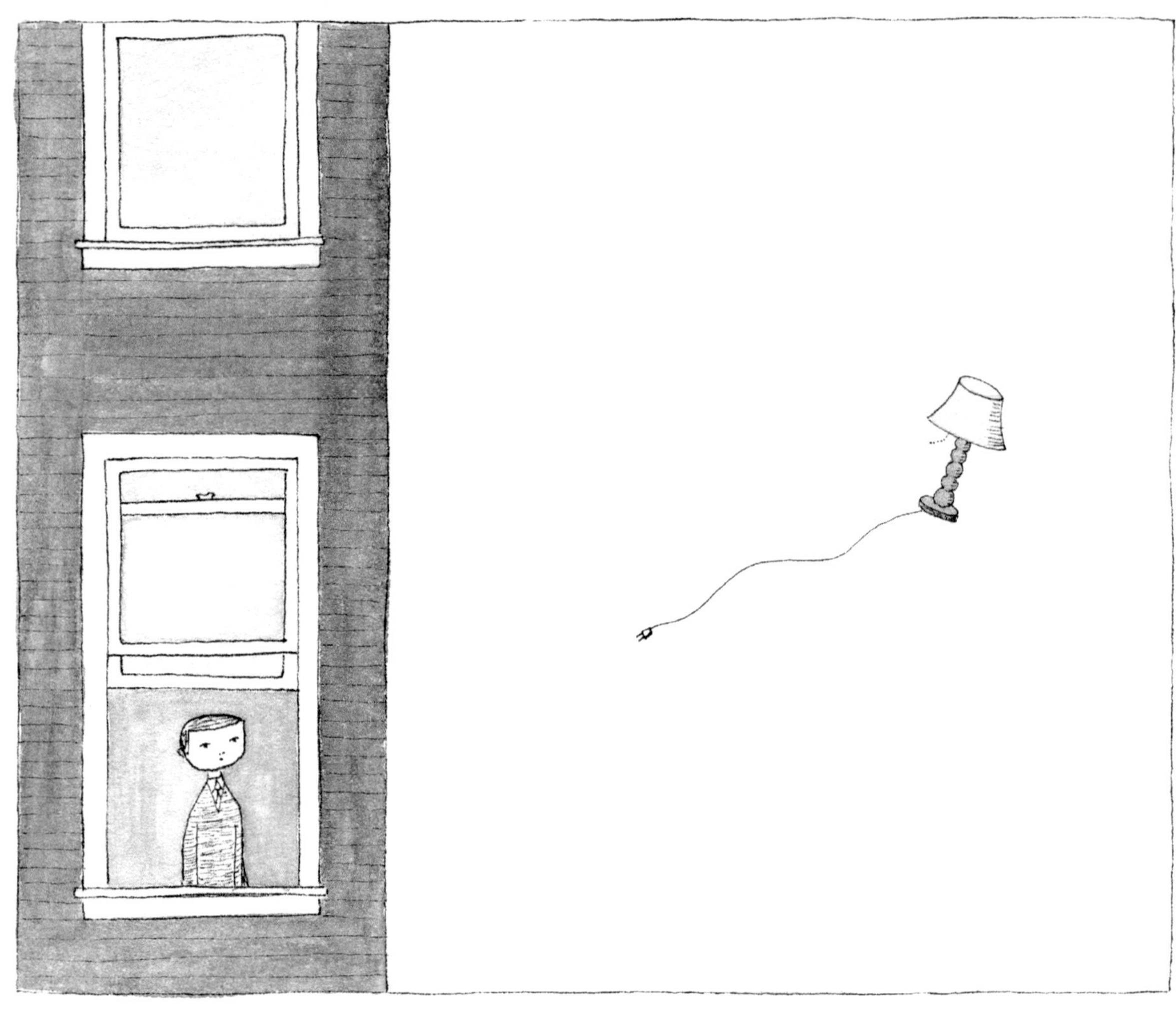

The bedside lamp, disgusted by the horrid selection of books that Mr. Denman insisted on reading lately, flew away in a huff.

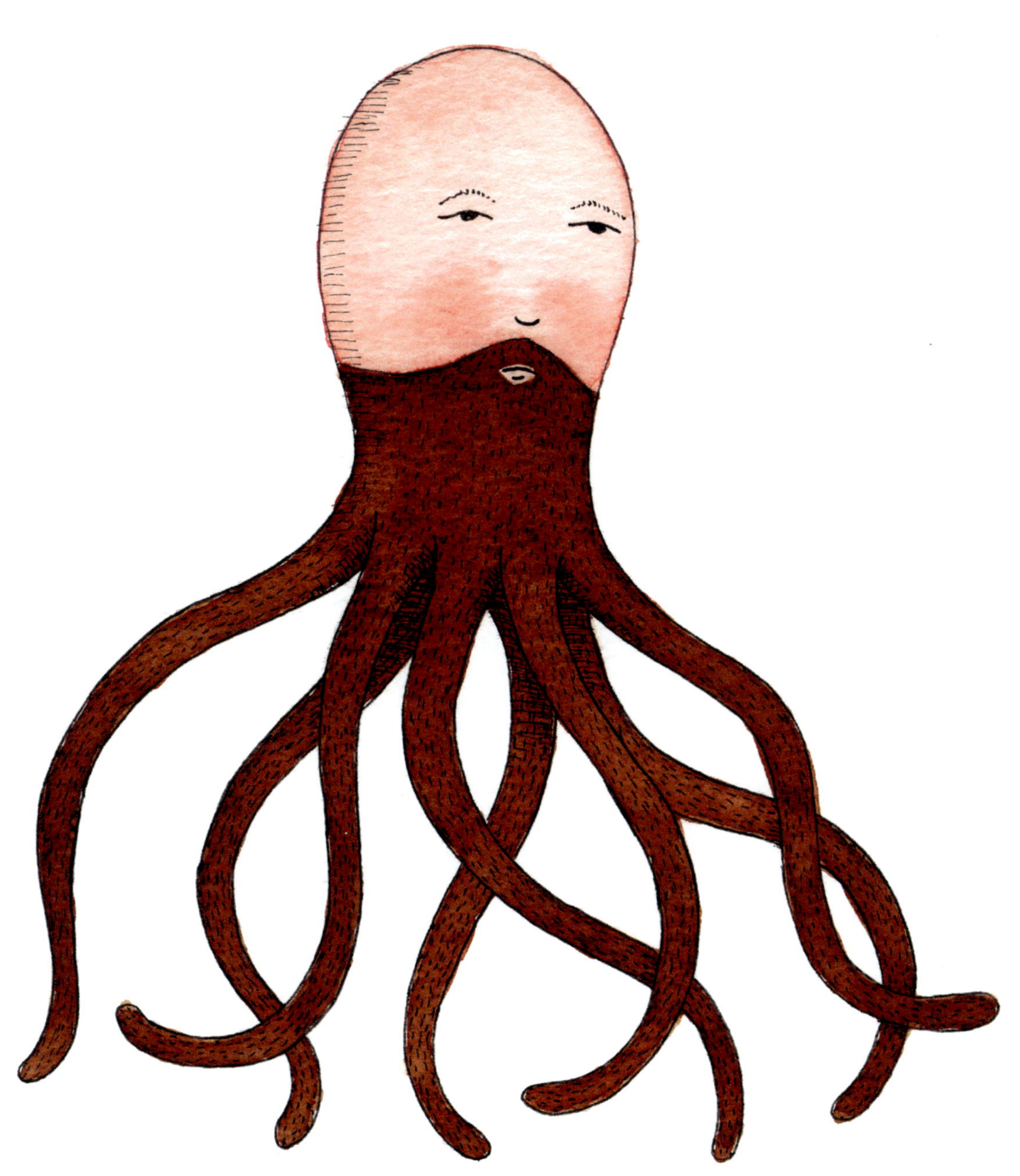

BEARD OCTOPUS

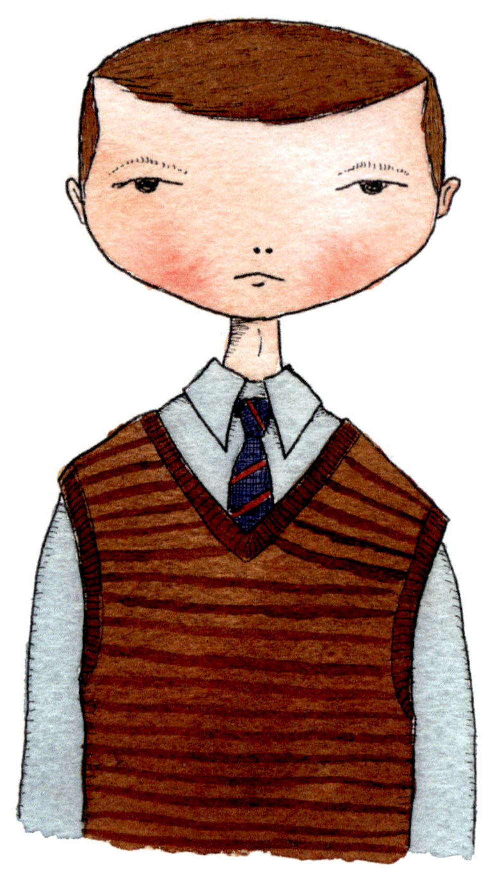

Tomorrow this man will obsess about things he cannot control for two hours instead of three.

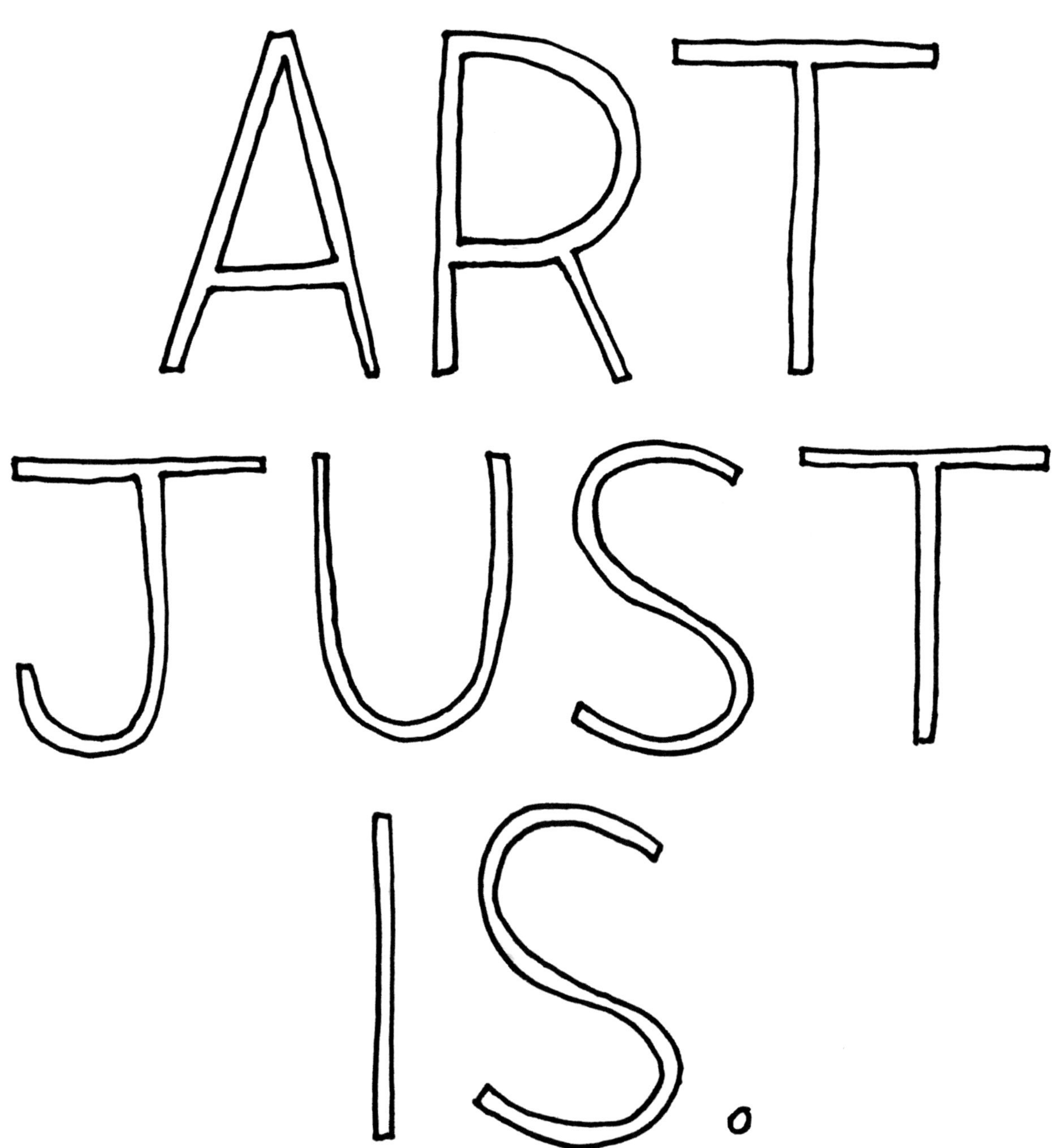
ART
JUST
IS.

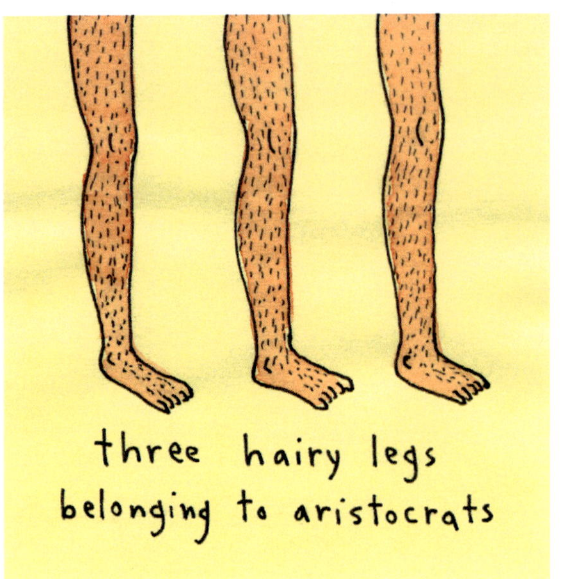
three hairy legs
belonging to aristocrats

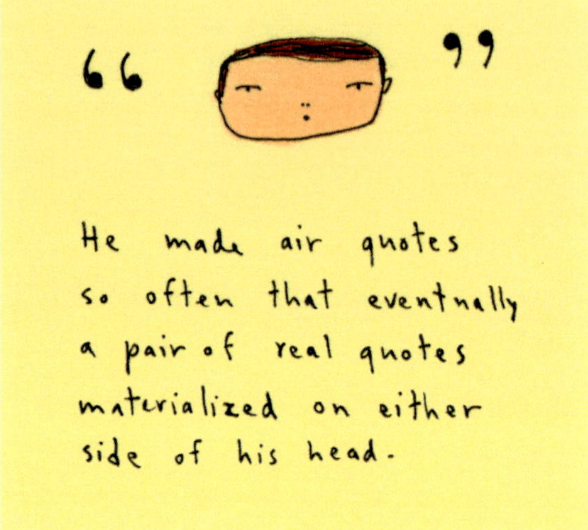
" "
He made air quotes
so often that eventually
a pair of real quotes
materialized on either
side of his head.

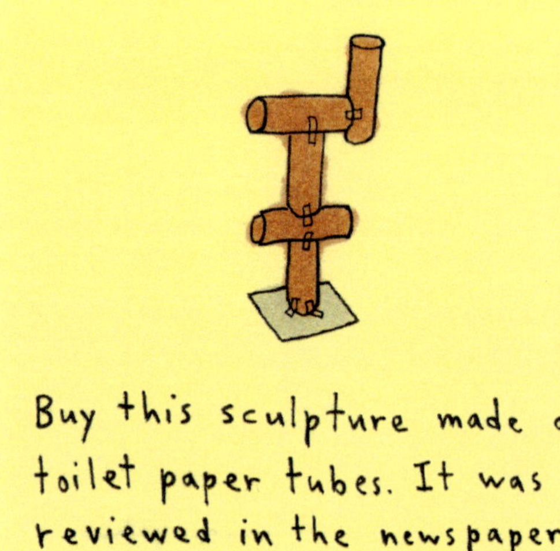
Buy this sculpture made of
toilet paper tubes. It was
reviewed in the newspaper.

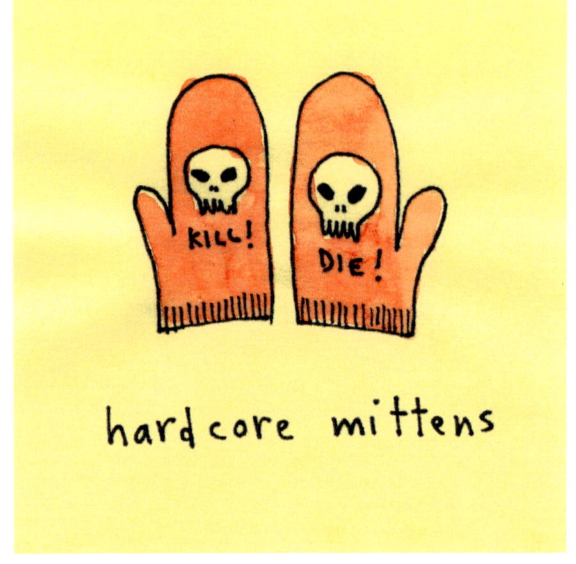
KILL!
DIE!
hardcore mittens

FERNS ON SALE

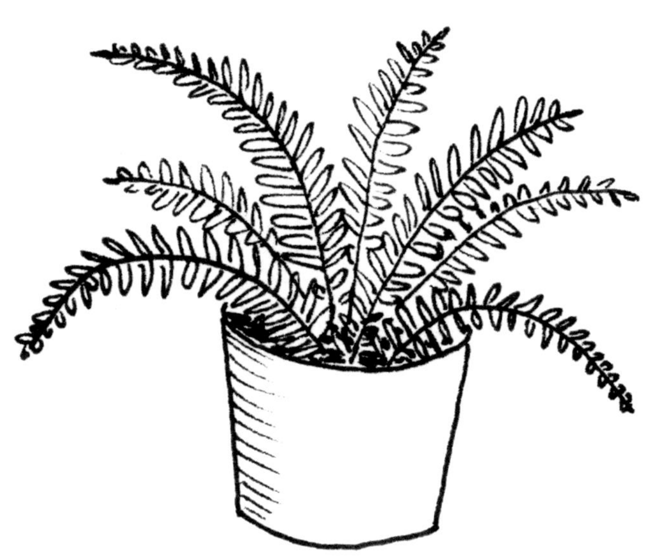

20% off if your name is Vern,

50% off if your name is Fern,

80% off if you happen to have

an autographed picture of Laura Dern.

He had a distinct advantage.

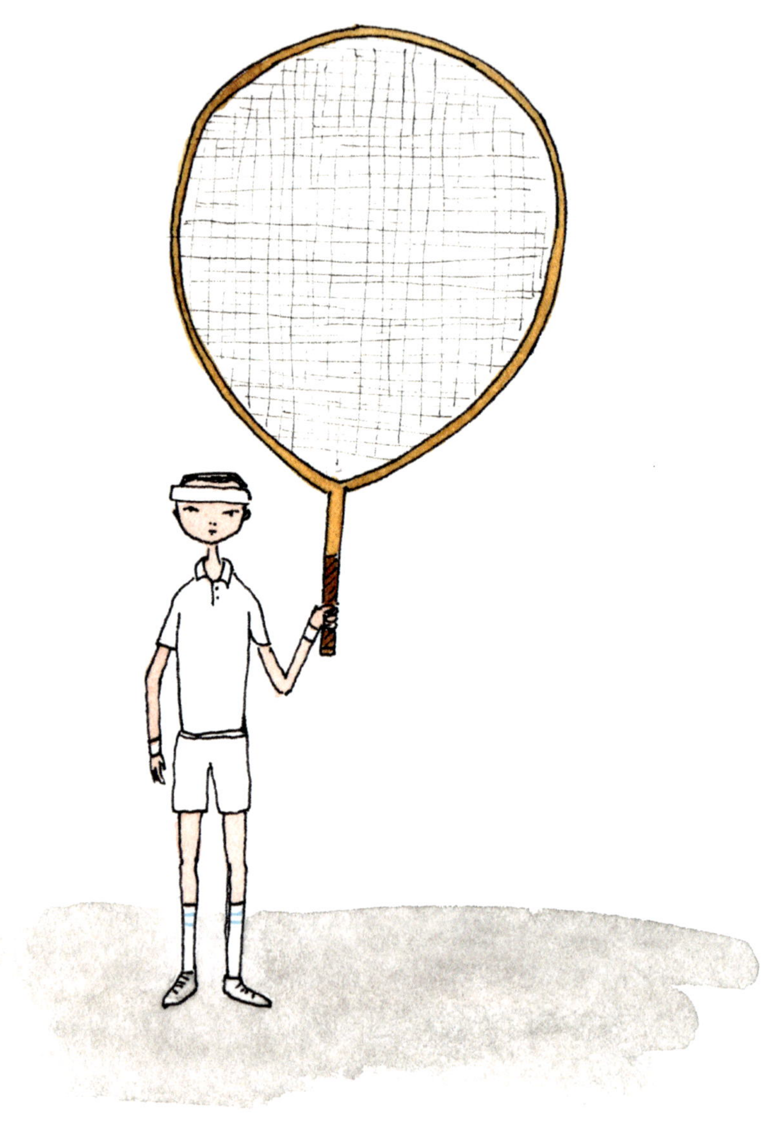

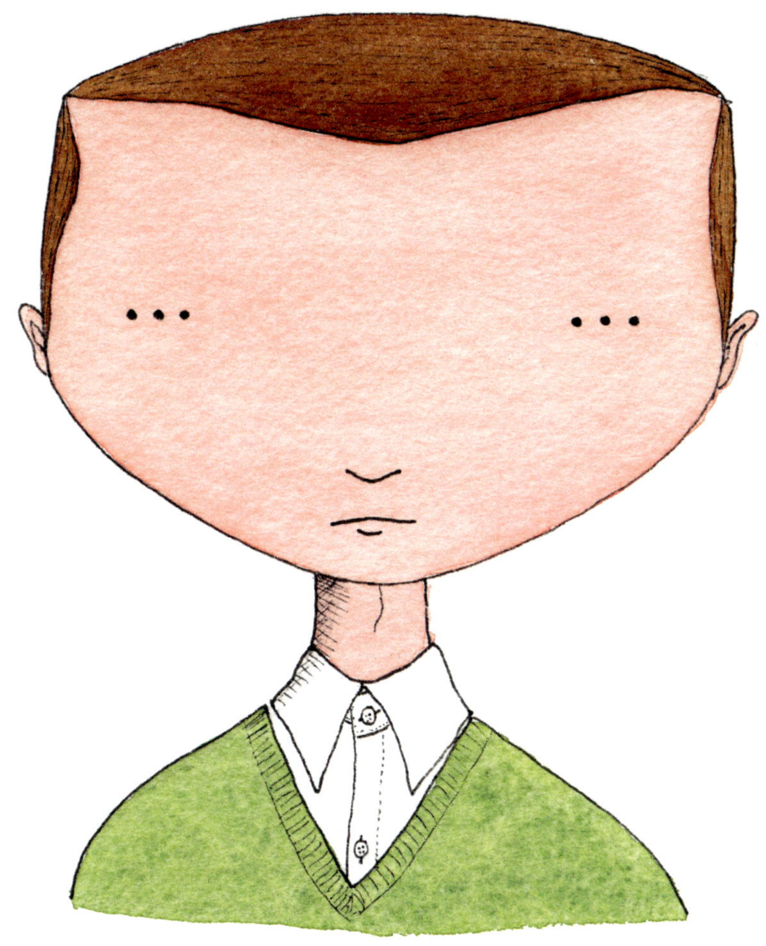

Many of Paul's friends from college had dollar signs in their eyes, but he preferred ellipses.

he collected branches
shaped like parentheses

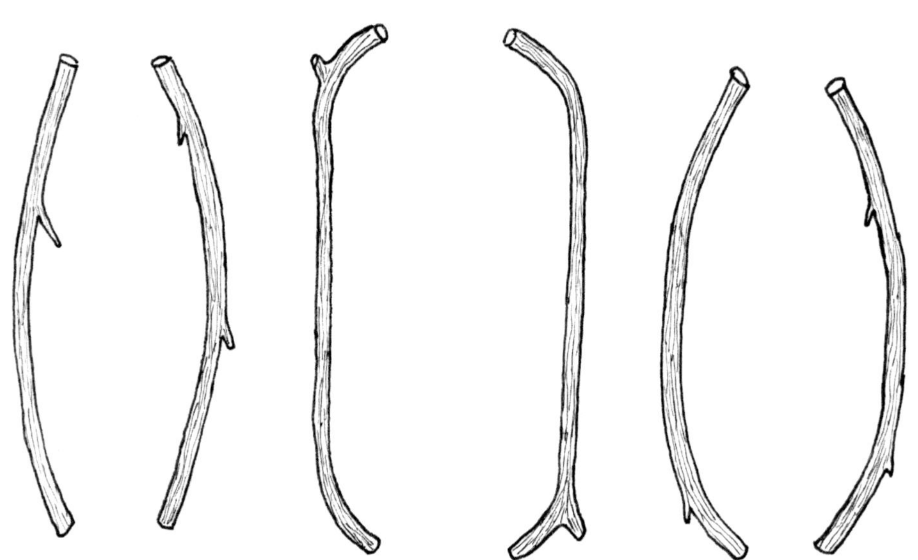

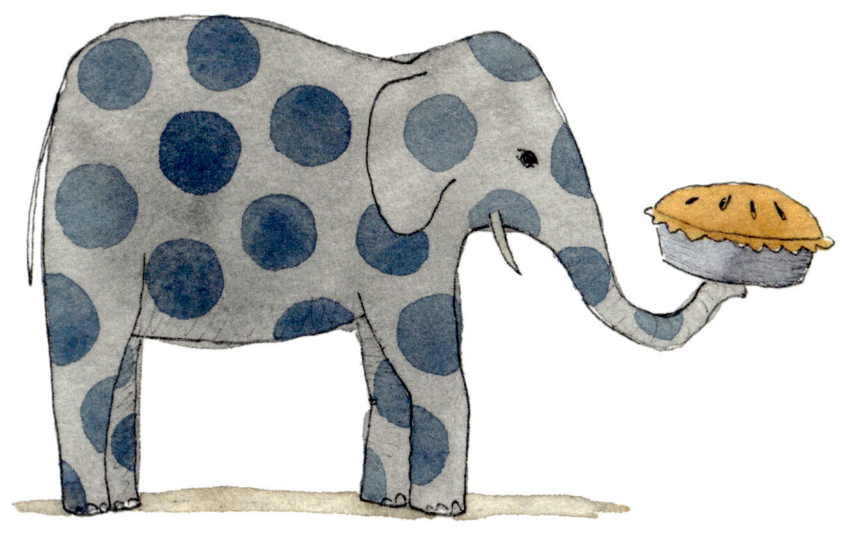

I'm truly surprised that we seem to get by
without polka dot elephants, serving us pie.

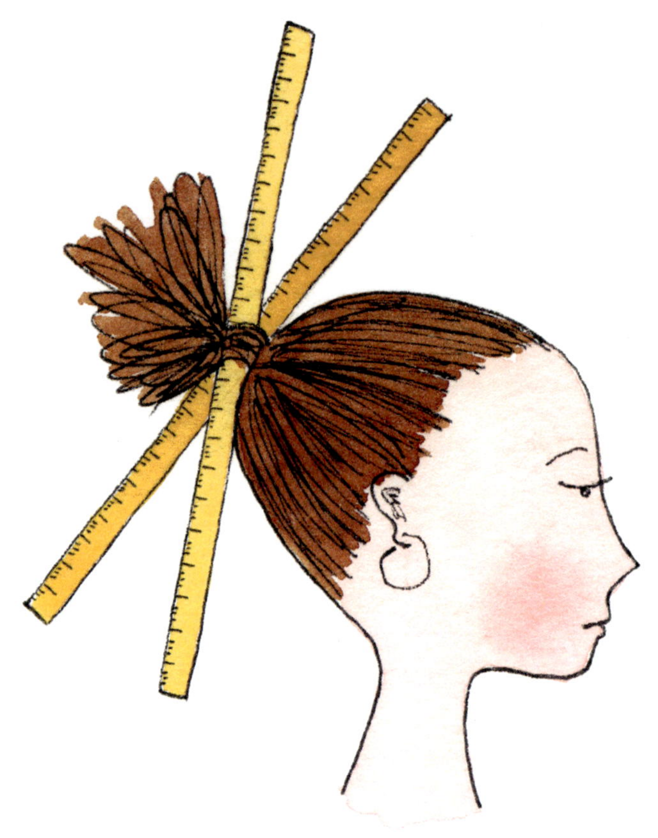

She was widely respected for her ability to incorporate rulers into her hairstyle.

a drawing of
a salt shaker

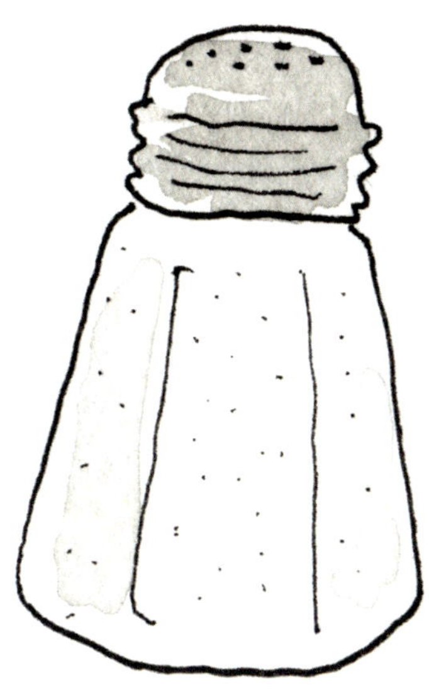

is more lovely
when surrounded
by stripes.

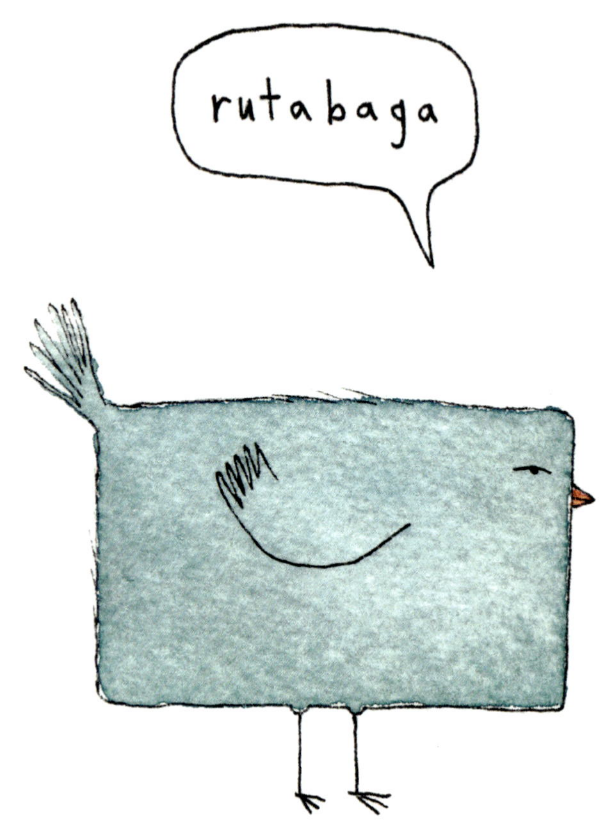

the rectangular bird
spoke only one word

HEY WORLD,
TALK TO ME
WHEN YOU
START MAKING
SOME GODDAMN
SENSE.

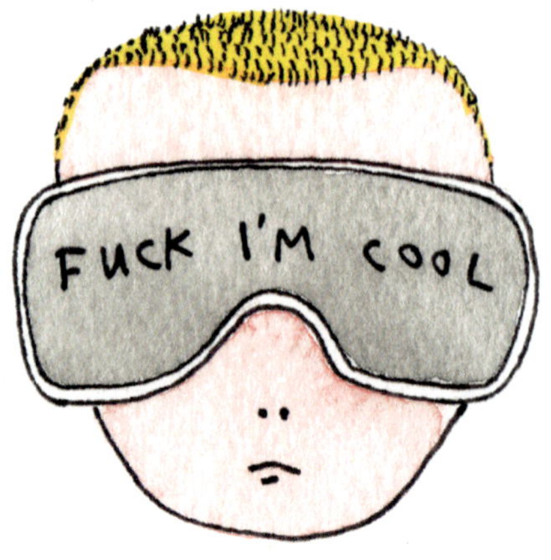
FUCK I'M COOL

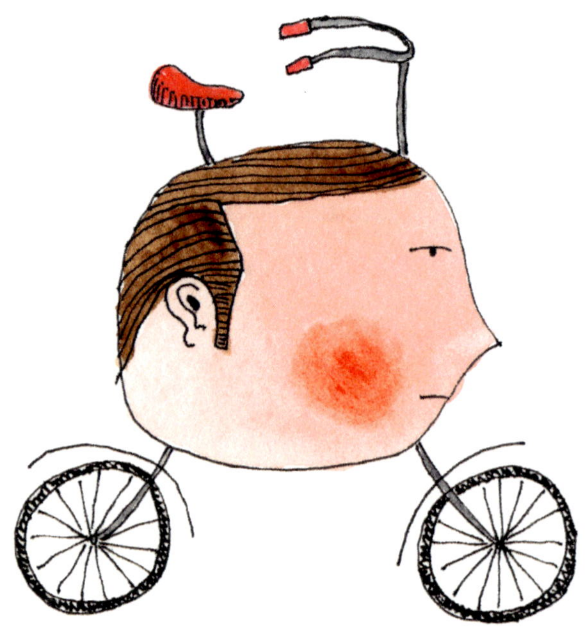

A FISH COSTUME

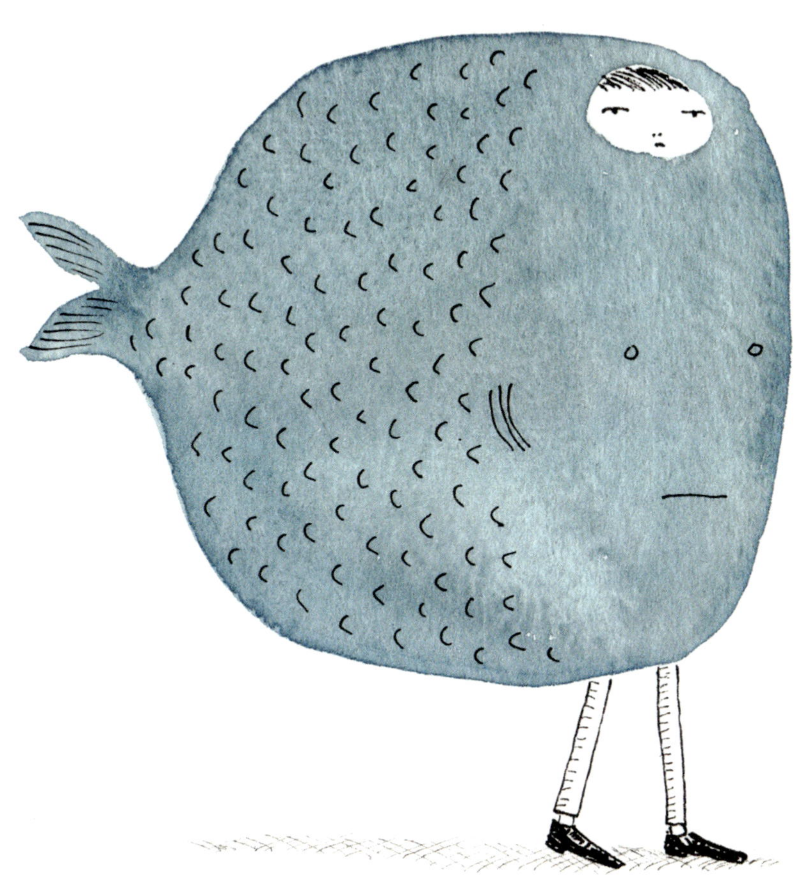

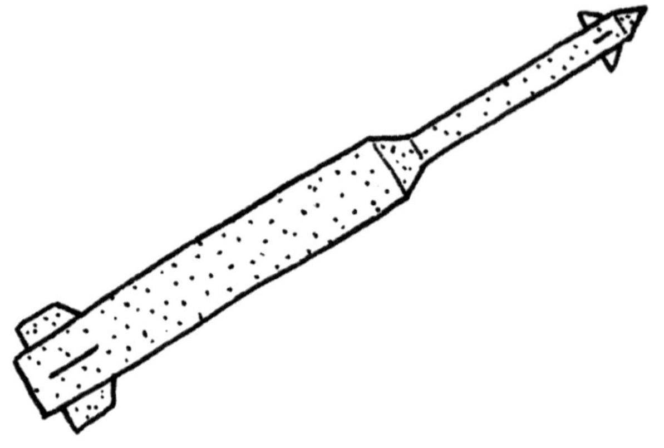

DIAMOND ENCRUSTED

INTERCONTINENTAL

BALLISTIC MISSILE

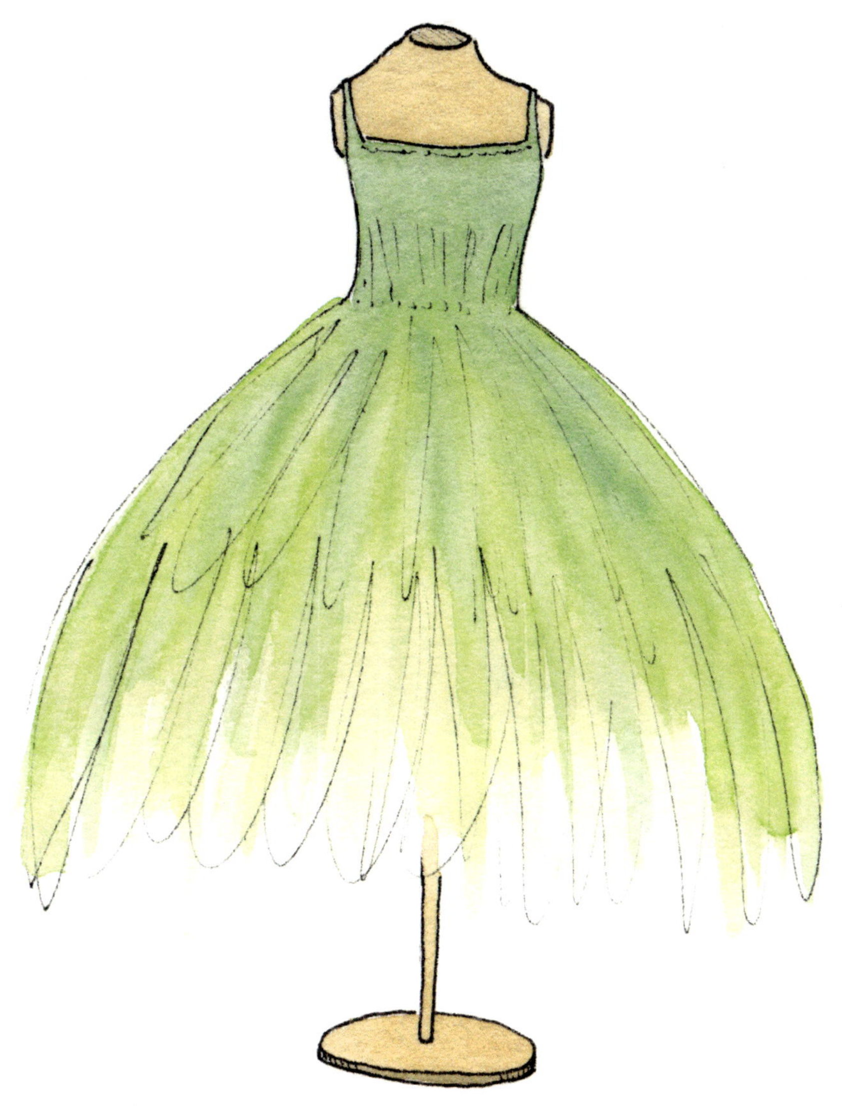

The dress looked much better on the headless, armless, legless mannequin.

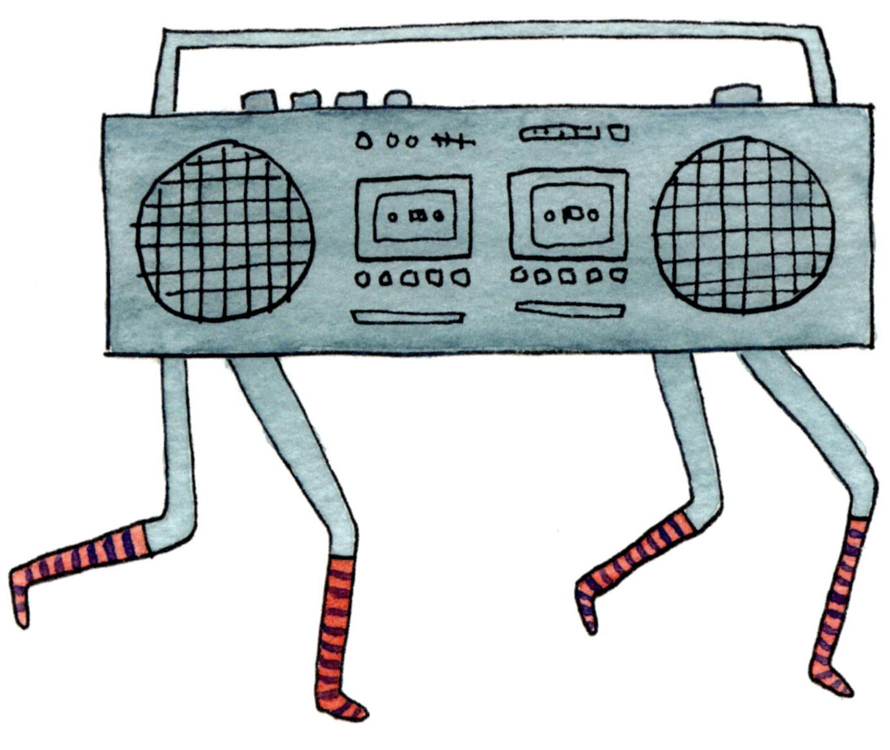

BOOM BOX IN STRIPED SOCKS

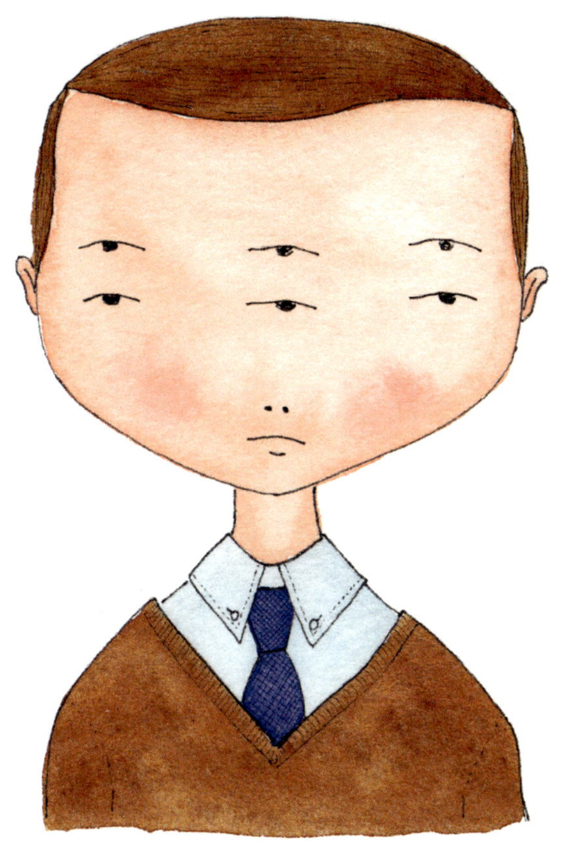

His eyes allowed him to become a member of the Men From June Who See Past December.

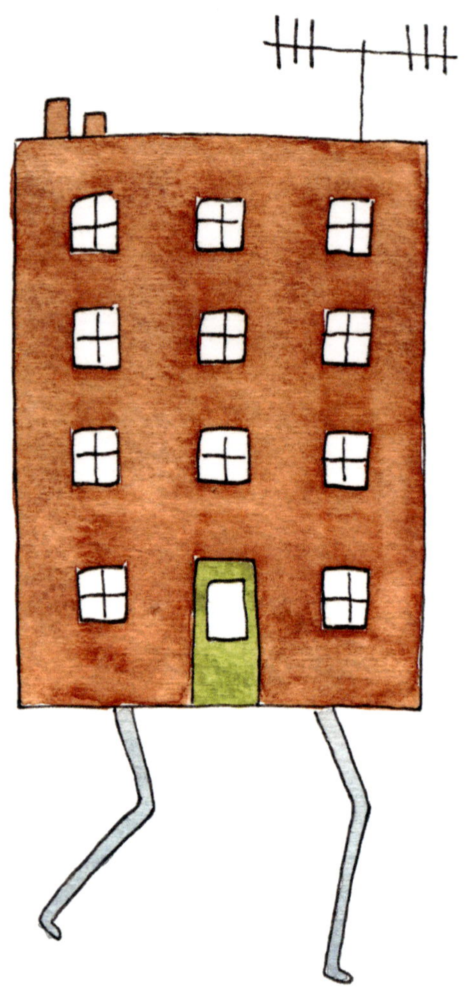

After a 100-year-long sleep, the four storey apartment building needed to stretch, so she went for a walk.

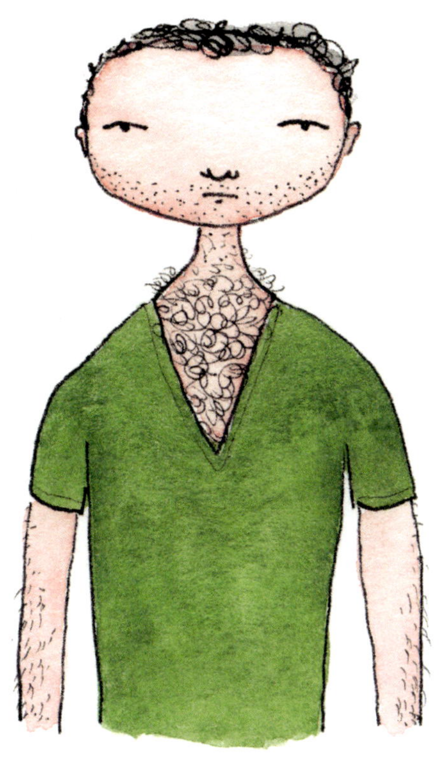

It is illegal to sell this man a v-neck t-shirt.

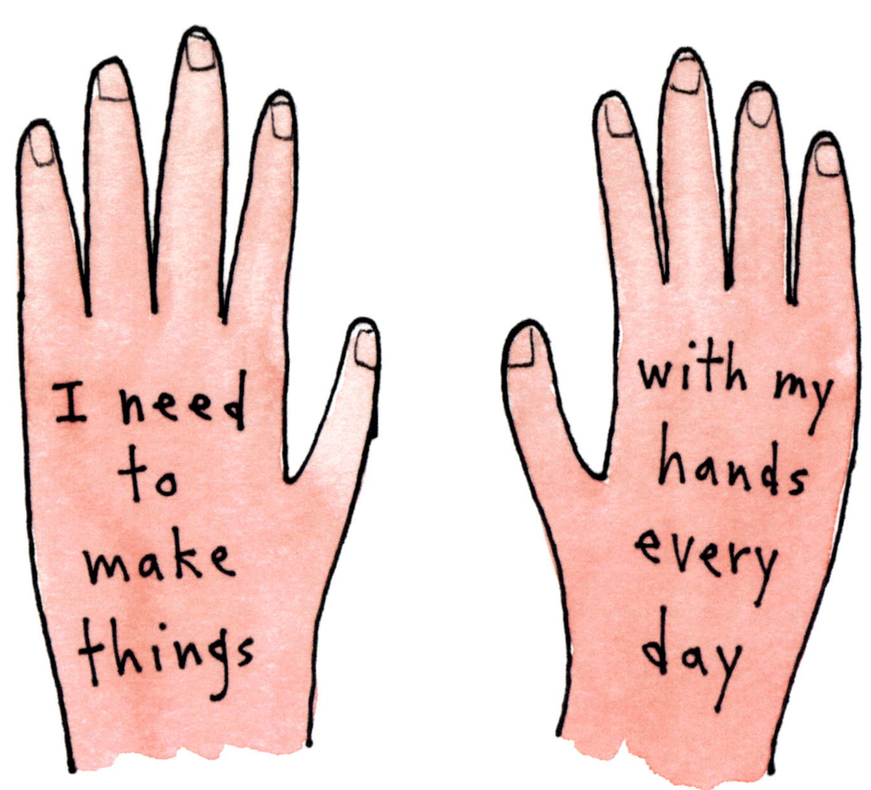
I need
to
make
things
with my
hands
every
day

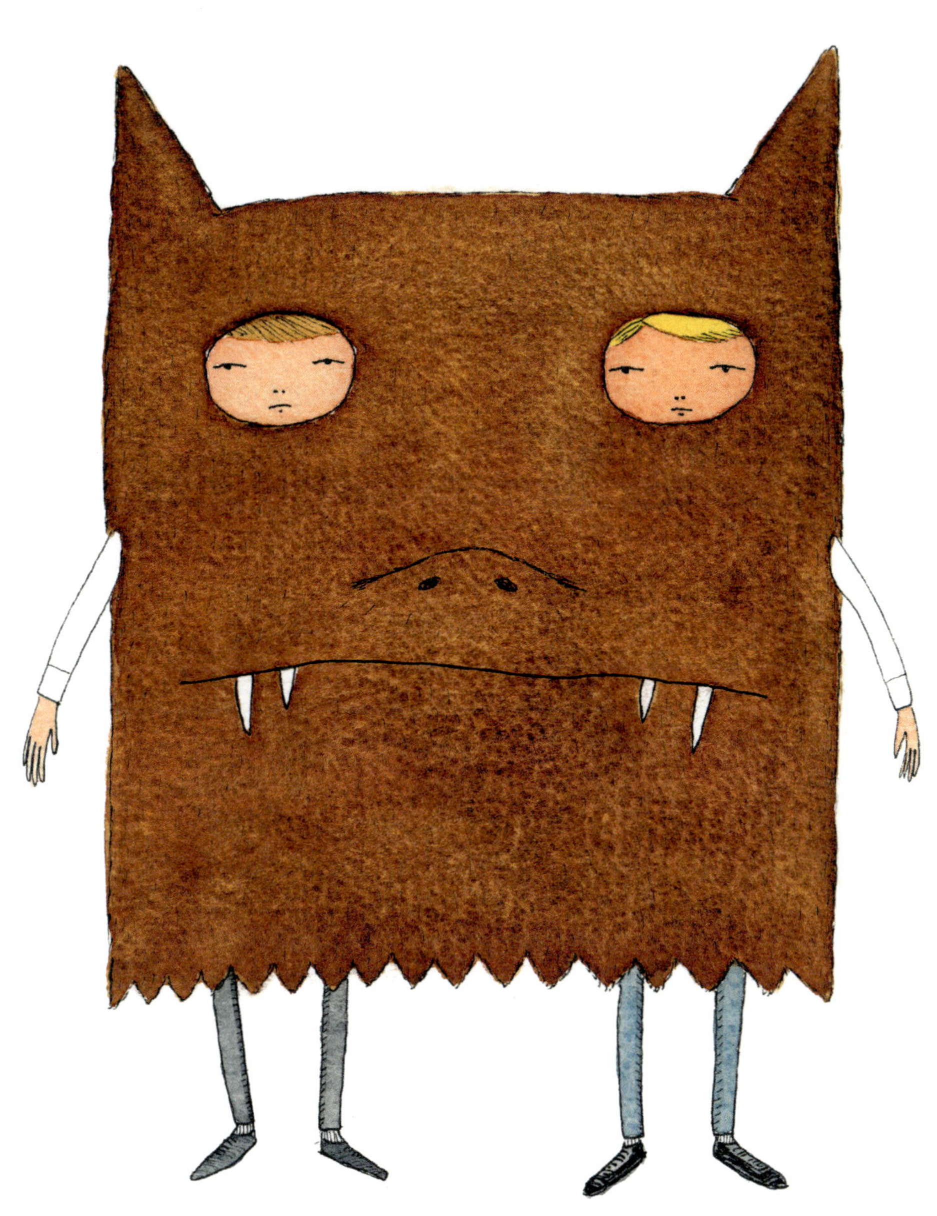

together we are fierce

ABOUT WHAT I DO

To me, the world doesn't make much sense, so there are plenty of absurdities to comment on. I don't think I'll ever run out of material. I try to make sense of it all, and the characters in my drawings are trying to make sense of it all, but they're not always sure how to proceed.

I get my ideas from everything and everywhere. I carry a small notebook and pen with me at all times, so that whenever an idea comes to mind I can get it on paper. I might be in a lineup at a coffee shop, on the bus, watching TV, or putting the kids to sleep. I'll overhear a conversation, see some quirky signage, spot an interesting pattern, or think of an odd combination of objects and I'll pull out a notebook and get the idea down on paper. Sometimes an idea for a drawing shows up in my head all ready to go. Other times it's just a single word, sometimes an object, a layout, which I come back to later to flesh out into something more complete. I have stacks of these little notebooks now, filled with mostly nonsense but with some (hopefully) decent ideas here and there. The drawings in them are super rough, sometimes unintelligible to anyone but me. But basically by the time I sit down with pens and watercolours, I know exactly what I'm going to make. When I don't know what to draw, I dig through my notebooks, and usually find something worthwhile.

I make my own notebooks. They're just regular office paper, cut down to size (to fit in my back pocket) and stapled together. Sometimes I make nice covers for them, sometimes I just use a bit of cardstock from a cereal box to keep them stiff. It's important for me that the notebook is not a precious thing. Using a fancy leather bound sketchbook with fine paper would be too restricting. It would make me filter my ideas, because I would only want the best drawings to go in it. It's vital that the idea generation process is unfiltered, free of judgement, that there are no wrong answers, and a million mistakes can be made with no cost (and therefore no risk) associated. Each notebook probably costs about 15 cents to make, and that keeps the whole process liberating and free-flowing.

My drawings often lean toward humour, and finding the humour in things often leads to finding the truth. I try to keep the drawings as simple as possible, and the humour a bit subtle, rather than deliver a punchline. I prefer dry humour, or humour delivered in a reserved fashion. I'd rather not spell it out.

ABOUT THE DRAWINGS IN THIS BOOK

All of the artwork in this book was created between 2009 and 2012 (except the drawings on paper towels on page 72). They are mostly reproduced at actual size. Some are made smaller, so that it's harder for you to see the flaws. Hey, it's my book so I can do whatever I want.

www.marcjohns.com

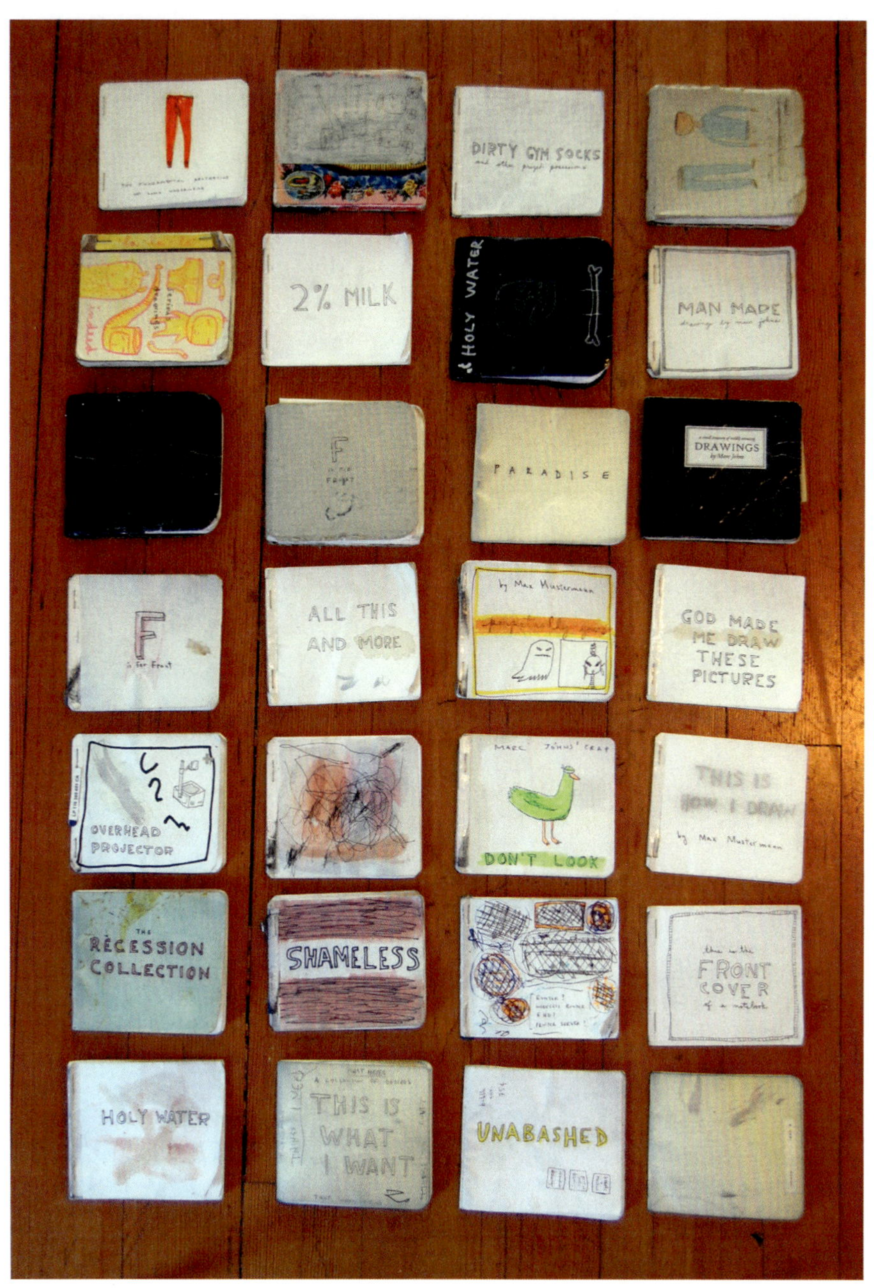

A selection of the dozens and dozens of notebooks I've made over the years.

EVERYTHING'S

GONNA BE

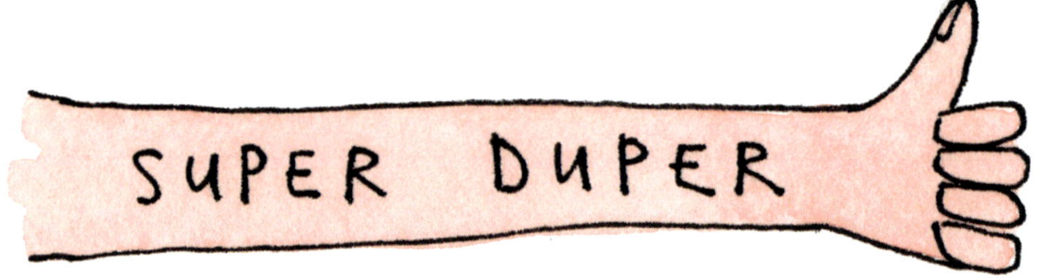

Made in the USA
Middletown, DE
08 July 2018